Understanding Perpetrators, Protecting Children

A practitioner's guide to working effectively with child sexual abusers

Lynda Deacon & Bryan Gocke
with Clark Baim and Dan Grant

Whiting & Birch
mcmxcix

© Lynda Deacon, Bryan Gocke, 1999
Chapter 8 © Dan Grant. Chapter 9 © Clark Baim
Published by Whiting & Birch Ltd,
    PO Box 872, London SE23 3HL, England.
    USA: Paul & Co, Publishers' Consortium Inc,
    PO Box 442, Concord, MA 01742.

British Library Cataloguing in Publication Data.
    A CIP catalogue record is available from
    the British Library

    ISBN 1 86177 022 7 (cased)
    ISBN 1 86177 021 9 (limp)

Illustrations to Chapter 9 by Reggie Freeman
Printed in England by Watkiss Studios

Contents

Introduction _____ ix
   The aims of this book _____ xiii

1 Theoretical background to child sex abuse _____ 1
   Organic theories _____ 2
   Psychodynamic and psychoanalytic theories _____ 3
   Family dysfunction theory _____ 5
   Behavioural theories _____ 10
   Feminist theory _____ 12
   Psychological/socio-cultural theories _____ 15
   Discussion _____ 18

2 How perpetrators abuse _____ 23
   Finkelhor's four stage model _____ 25
   Finkelhor's four factor framework _____ 29
   Wolf's multi-factor model _____ 31

3 How to work with perpetrators _____ 39
   Denial _____ 40
   Working with denial _____ 43
   Triggers _____ 45
   Masturbation and fantasy _____ 45
   Grooming _____ 46
   The abuse _____ 48
   Victim empathy _____ 49
   Changes to be encouraged in abusers _____ 50
   Relapse prevention _____ 51
   Rehabilitation _____ 53
   Supervision and support _____ 57

4 Assessment of risk in family situations _____ 60
   Risk and sexual abusers _____ 61
   Assessing risk: What is the nature of the task? _____ 64
   What can be expected of risk assessments ? _____ 66
   Ways of assessing risk _____ 67
   Models for assessing risk _____ 69

5 Multifactor approaches to the assessment of risk
   and risk management _____ 72
   Basic information _____ 74
   Offending history _____ 75
   Analysis of abusive behaviour _____ 76
   Analysis of current circumstances _____ 81
   Conclusions and assessment of risk _____ 86

6 Assessment of risk: Examples _____ 90
   Basic information on two scenarios _____ 90
   Assessment of known abusive behaviour _____ 93
   Assessment of current and proposed future circumstances _ 95
   Conclusions for the two scenarios _____ 98
   Final observations _____ 101

7 Assessment processes _____ 102
   The context within which assessments of risk take place _ 103
   Supervision of workers undertaking risk assessment _____ 104
   Who should undertake assessments? _____ 107
   Establishing and maintaining co-working relationships __ 108
   The professional role _____ 111
   Planning risk assessments _____ 112
   Engaging subjects in the assessment process _____ 116
   Methods _____ 120
   Working with difference _____ 123
   Report writing _____ 130
   Risk assessments and multi-agency working _____ 132
   Assessment of risk with absolute denial _____ 132
   Basic information _____ 133
   Analysis of abusive behaviour _____ 133
   Abuser's sexual motivation to abuse _____ 134
   Overcoming internal inhibitors _____ 134
   Circumventing external inhibitors _____ 134
   Overcoming victim resistance _____ 134
   Analysis of current circumstances _____ 135
   Abuser's current sexual motivations _____ 135
   Abuser's maintenance of internal controls _____ 135
   Effectiveness of external controls _____ 135
   Potential victims _____ 135
   Risk assessment: A task worth doing _____ 136

8 **Change, monitoring and containment: A selective**
  overview of the nature and efficacy of professional
  interventions with child sexual abusers _____ 137
  Cognitive-behavioural type treatment programmes for child
  sexual abusers _____ 138
  Case Study 1: Mick _____ 140
  Effectiveness research: Do sex offender treatment
  programmes work? _____ 146
  Types of offender _____ 146
  Length of programme _____ 147
  Therapeutic tasks _____ 147
  Impressions of success in therapy _____ 148
  Relapse prevention _____ 148
  Programme implementation and management _____ 149
  Relapse prevention with child sexual abusers _____ 150
  Monitoring behaviour _____ 154
  Family and community support _____ 154
  Networking _____ 154
  Controlling child sexual abusers in the community:
  Multi-agency risk management _____ 155
  Case Study 2: Charlie _____ 156
  Intervening without statutory authority:
  Working with unconvicted child sexual abusers _____ 161
  Case Study 3: Ron _____ 163

9 **Techniques in supervision for those working**
  with sexual abusers _____ 166
  Introduction _____ 166
  Supervision in working with abusers _____ 167
  About the techniques described here _____ 169
  Structuring supervision:
  Content, process and feelings _____ 170
  Two final points about role reversal and role play _____ 173
  One: Outer Face/ Inner World _____ 174
  Two: Past, present and future _____ 177
  Three: The hypothetical sex offender interview _____ 179
  Four: One person, many roles _____ 181
  Five: Social networks _____ 183
  Six: Objects and empty chairs _____ 185

References _____ 187

Introduction

CHILD SEXUAL abuse is a worrying feature of our society. Since the mid 1980s this area of social work has been a significant feature of the caseloads of social workers in Children and Families Teams. More and more probation officers are finding that they have to work with schedule 1 sexual offenders, just as housing support workers are finding an increase in the number of perpetrators of sexual abuse in their housing projects.

Research of recent years provides a varied picture of the amount of sexual abuse perpetrated in the UK This is because researchers often define what constitutes sexual abuse in very different ways. The following examples are of note: Nash and West (1985) surveyed 223 GP patients between the ages of 20 and 39. They used both questionnaires and face to face interviews. The response rate was 53%. The survey found that 42% of the respondents had been subject to non-contact sexual abuse, whilst 22% had been recipients of sexual abuse involving contact.

BBC Childwatch (1986) sent questionnaires to almost 3,000 males and females who had written in requesting them. The return rate was 75%, and 90% of the respondents stated that they had been sexually abused.

Baker and Duncan (1985) sampled 2,019 men and women by conducting face to face interviews in the respondents' home. They had an 87% response rate and found that 12% of the females and 8% of the males had been subject to non-contact sexual abuse. In terms of sexual abuse involving contact, 5% of the females and 4% of males had been abused.

The 1987 BBC Childwatch National Interview Survey sampled 2,041 adults over the age of 16. The results of this survey found that 3% of the sample had suffered child sexual abuse involving contact.

Kelly et al. (1991) surveyed 1,244 polytechnic students aged between 16 and 25 years. They were given a questionnaire in the classroom, the response rate was 97%. The results showed 59% of the women and 27% of the men had been subjected to non-contact abuse whilst 27% of women and 11% of men had suffered child sexual abuse involving contact.

Finkelhor et al (1990) conducted a telephone interview with 2,626 adults. The response rate was 76% and the results showed 27% of women and 16% of men had been sexually abused, most of them by contact offences.

To put the prevalence rates into context, we must look at the figures for sexual abuse in the framework of child abuse as a whole. Sexual abuse accounts for around 15% of all abuse cases according to some sources (*Children and young people on Child Protection Registers for the year ending 31 March 1992, England*; 1993 figures from the Department of Health, 1993; and the figures from the Association of Directors of Social Work, *Scottish Child Abuse Statistics, 198*)). The statistics for Wales indicate 11%. For Scotland the overall rate per 1.000 for all types of child abuse is 2.01. For Wales it is 2.15, and for England, 2.25. These are not insignificant figures. Research informs us that child sexual abuse is likely to be under-reported—these are just the children we know about.

For every child abused there is a perpetrator. The Home office Research Findings No.55, *The Prevalence of Convictions for Sexual Offending*, (1997) tells us that in 1996 4,426 offenders were convicted and 2,027 were cautioned for indictable sexual offences. These included rape, indecent assault, unlawful sexual intercourse, indecency between males and gross indecency with a child. In the same year, 1,185 offenders were convicted of indecent exposure (a non-contact sexual offence) and 187 men were cautioned for the same.

All statistics relating to the level of conviction for sexual offences must be seen in the light of the fact that many such offences are not reported and only a minority of those that are reported result in prosecution and conviction. Many social workers will be aware of cases in the Family Courts where in Care Proceedings the Judge has made a 'Finding of Fact' against a parent or step-parent naming them as the perpetrator of child sexual abuse. However, for many reasons the majority of these cases do not go to criminal proceedings, and, if they do, the charge is often reduced to a less serious offence by an effective defence lawyer. Some cases do not go to court because the Criminal Prosecution Service tend not to pursue cases where the child is very young. This is sometimes because a young child may not be considered a good witness, and sometimes because it is felt that it would not be in their best interest to undergo cross examination by the defence barrister. It is our experience that young children can give good evidence, but that a system that subjects young children to combative cross examination needs to be changed.

Home Office research figures for 1993 state that 110,000 people, mostly men, had a conviction for an offence against a child. A study of 3,947 offenders against children found that 20% were convicted of an indictable sex offence and 16% of a child sex offence (Soothill, Francis and Ackerley, 1998).

Although most child sexual abusers are male, females can and do sexually abuse children. The studies give different prevalence rates for female sex abusers. It is estimated that up to 20% of abusers of boys and 5% of abusers of girls are women. In some cases the abuse is carried out in conjunction with a male abuser, or because the woman is forced to carry this out as part of her own sexual abuse by a male. However in a recent study of 127 cases of abuse by females, 75% of the victims said that they had been abused by females acting alone (Elliot, 1993). Richards (1990) found that women could abuse as sadistically as men and that the general view that women's abuse of children was more gentle and less damaging was a fallacy.

Childhood Matters (1996) Vols 1&2 published by the National Commission of Inquiry into the Prevention of Child Abuse looked at over 1,000 letters received from victims of child sexual abuse. In 40% of cases the abusers were fathers or stepfathers; 30% were other relatives known to the child; 5% were friends, neighbours or substitute cares; and 4% were teachers, doctors, priests or lodgers. Moreover a total of 91% of the victims knew their abuser. Of course the media do not report these statistics when they run emotive stories about child sex abusers and paedophiles, who are portrayed as operating on the fringes of society. Statistically children are more at risk from child sexual abuse in their own home than from a stranger while they are outside playing.

Child sexual abuse can have long-term effects on the victims. A minority can in turn become abusers. The majority may suffer a myriad of effects, such as mental health problems, self-harming and suicide attempts, violence and aggression, misuse of alcohol and drugs, relationship problems and problems with parenting. Child sexual abuse exacts a social, psychological, emotional and economic cost from our society.

This book has come from the authors combined experience of working with child sex abusers. Both the editors and the contributing authors have considerable experience in working in the field and the good fortune to have received specialist training. For all of us it was a conscious decision to enter the field but the routes taken were different.

Lynda Deacon began as a Children and Families Social worker and then became a GP attached social worker over 11 years ago having completed research into the then unpopular field of female perpetrators of sexual abuse. With no prior warning or preparation, she was asked to work with a man who had abused his 12 year old daughter. The Crown Prosecution Service were not bringing charges, and his wife believed him and not her daughter. Lynda found herself in a room with a man who described himself as a 'stallion' and felt no shame or responsibility for raping his 12 year old daughter. She felt out of her depth, she knew she was being manipulated but could not work out how.

She asked for help (this is an understatement she shouted very loudly) and was fortunate enough to be heard by an experienced worker on a large groupwork programme. He worked with her, supervised her and gave her a crash course in the theories that inform work of this kind. She later worked on the same programme for four years and now remembers thanking him when he left the programme on promotion. He was surprised. For him it had just been another case. For Lynda it was seminal in that she realised that there was a knowledge base out there that could inform her work and moreover help her to protect children.

Since then, Lynda has worked for Social Service Departments as a practitioner, manager and trainer. She is now Director of Practice Teaching at Sheffield University and also works as Staff Tutor in Social Work for the Open University managing the Diploma in Social Work programme for the Northern Region. She has also worked for the NSPCC for the last seven years.

Bryan Gocke first came into professional contact with abusers in the early 1980s when working in direct access emergency accommodation for men. Other residents and part of the staff group were hostile to the agency's providing a service to sexual offenders. This felt instinctively wrong to him, but he had to concede that the agency knew little at that time about the issues and risks posed by abusers.

Bryan's attempts to explore these matters generated, what was for him, at that time, startling information: sexual abuse is a significant social problem which is largely denied or minimised; abusers often victimise a number of people many times: and they are overwhelmingly male. The latter point was, and still is, an uncomfortable revelation and further research revealed that sexual abusers are not in many respects markedly different from other men (including Bryan himself!) He could no longer view sexual abusers as being fundamentally different and was forced to make the links between his own sexism and the behaviour of those men who sexually assault. Attempting to take some responsibility for contributing to changing this appalling state of affairs has been a major motivation in Bryan's development of a degree of specialism in this area of work. He has subsequently worked for the Probation Service and a local authority social services department as a practitioner, manager and trainer. He continues to operate a small independent practice as a consultant and trainer.

The aims of this book

Working with child sex abusers can be difficult. However, if we as workers arm ourselves with the correct tools, receive sufficient support for the work and the impact issues that come with it, then we can do it. We can more effectively protect children and grow professionally and personally.

This book is dedicated to the front line workers, the ones who are doing 95% of the work with child abusers, those who are struggling to deliver high quality work with little or no training in the field whilst still carrying a 'normal' social services or probation case load. It is for those workers within housing associations who see more and more perpetrators within their client base. Often neither these workers nor their supervisors are qualified social workers, yet the demands of the job means that they are increasingly being asked to act as key workers to Schedule 1 sexual abusers.

This book intends to give the reader the information and tools to begin to work with child sex abusers. It is not our intention that this book should replace training, or the development over time of skills. It is seen as a starting point for workers who need to ensure that they are able to access the ongoing training and support that is necessary for this work, and to have an understanding of the work carried out by specialist colleagues.

We will look at the theories which have been developed to help explain and understand child sex abuse. We will explore how perpetrators typically operate and then move on to the consider the assessment of risk and how children may be safeguarded. We do this because at all times in this work we must assess and manage the risk posed to children. Dan Grant will look at change, monitoring and containment. Dan is a probation officer who undertook research in this area for his PhD at Hull University. He specialises in risk in the community and brings a thoughtful approach to all his work. Clark Baim is an independent psychodramatist, group psychotherapist and trainer specialising in work with violent and sexually abusive offenders. He has put together some creative suggestions and exercises to use in supervision. These are based upon the pioneering work of the Geese Theatre Company of which he was founder and formerly Artistic Director. Geese Theatre Company work with drama in the field, both with workers and perpetrators. The techniques used are a powerful way of understanding the complexity of child sexual abuse. We can also attest that the workshops and training sessions are fun!

Many people have wittingly or unwittingly contributed to this book. Many of them belong to the National Organisation for the Treatment of Abusers (NOTA), an organisation that gives support, training and information to its members. It is a lively forum for debate and the interchange of ideas. We would like to thank all the members who have contributed to the development of our combined knowledge. Needless to say we are all active members.

Professional issues in the management of sexually abusive behaviour will be explored. The context and the conditions required for safe working, including co-working and multi-agency working will be considered. Concerns about professional dangerousness are addressed, in particular the role of management in providing good quality supervision which allows consideration of all the issues germane to this area of work.

Finally we consider personal impact issues. We will look at the importance of support networks and the effects of 'grooming' on workers. The issues raised by gender in co-working or supervision relationships are given importance, particularly the question of male power and the need for men to address this openly and honestly. Research by Lynda Deacon into this issue will be discussed as will information gained from seminars on the issue presented by both Bryan and Lynda. Issues of sexuality and keeping safe will also be discussed.

We are aware as writers and practitioners that this work carries a cost in terms of impact issues. Working with difference in an area that makes for the questioning of fundamentally held values requires the ability to treat perpetrators with respect and humanity. This can often cause difficulties and lead to stress for workers who may also be providing therapeutic and protective services for children who were victims and are now moving along the continuum of victim-survivor-thrivor. There can be costs for workers in their personal lives as workers new to the field, in particular men begin to look at their own socialisation and how this affects their gender relations. Moreover working with either the perpetrator or survivor of sexual abuse can have a detrimental affect on the worker's libido, partners need to be aware of this and of the possible impact on the relationship discussed at the commencement of the work.

We will look at these issues in greater depth later in the book. It is now the time to move on and begin to look at how perpetrators work and how professionals can use this information in an attempt to make our children safer.

Conclusion

The aim of this book is therefore to enhance the public protection of children. The objectives include:

• giving workers the information they need to begin to work with perpetrators

- developing an understanding of risk assessment, management and containment
- suggesting some tools to be used in supervision
- developing an initial understanding of impact issues
- looking at how workers can keep themselves safe.

Chapter 1

Theoretical background to child sex abuse

CURRENT THINKING suggests increasing confidence in our ability to manage and work with child sexual abusers within the community, provided that the risk of re-abusing has been assessed at 'medium to low'. Of course, most people convicted and imprisoned for sexual offences where the risk is assessed as high will also require supervision and monitoring within the community. In the past five years there has been an upsurge in community programmes for perpetrators of child sex abuse. The STEP report published in 1994, looked at six community programmes of various sizes and one residential programme during 1992 and 1993, and concluded that group programmes were successful provided that they were long-term and intensive. It was also found that the treatment programmes needed to include relapse prevention and that the assessment process needed to be rigorous to ensure that only those perpetrators were chosen who displayed a risk that it was safe to manage in the community.

However little attention has been given to the work undertaken in the community by singleton social workers, probation officers, housing workers and community psychiatric nurses. Often the assumption is that the work will take place in a specialist group work setting where there are varying degrees of training and support for the workers. Hudson (1994) and Waterhouse (1993) argue that 95% of work with child sex abusers is not undertaken in supported groupwork settings but by practitioners in various disciplines working on their own and often with a less than satisfactory level of supervision. Whilst this work can be challenging and exciting, leading to personal and professional development, it is at times a source of pressure and stress. A good understanding of the context in which practitioners operate is essential if such difficulties are to remain manageable.

In this chapter we look at the development over recent years of theory that has been or is used to explain child sexual abuse. This is not an exhaustive account and readers will hopefully feel encouraged to do further reading on the subject.

Wattam et al (1988) states that child sexual abuse is a

> ... *diverse assortment of medical, psychiatric, feminist, legal and sociological conceptions, not to mention the diversity introduced by varying moral stances, the lack of well defined and widely accepted symptomology, and the sheer range of possible behaviours that could be construed as child sexual abuse.*

There are many contributions to the literature of child sexual abuse both from practice and research. In order to understand the developments in thinking it is interesting to look briefly at the evolution of the theories used to explain child sexual abuse, and in particular the behaviours of men who abuse children. It is worth noting at this stage that many of the theories and explanations hold to the idea that treatment can only be undertaken when the abuser or alleged abuser takes full responsibility for their actions. Bentovim, Elton and Tranter, 1987; Dale, Davies Morrison and Waters, 1986). We do not agree with this premise; there is work that can be done with abusers to get them to a stage when they can begin to look at the complex issue of responsibility.

Organic theories

This school of thought has few supporters and, in our opinion, is based on very little empirical evidence. Despite this, some commentators have argued that the cause of sexual offending is to be found in biological or organic deficits or irregularities. For example Langevin (1990) claims that there is a link between 'temporal lobe impairment' and irregular sexual behaviour. This theory is based upon small studies of men and conclude that there is a causal factor in sexual abuse because of high levels of testosterone resulting in high sex drives. None of these theories adequately address why this should cause some men to sexually abuse children rather than engage in sex with adult partners or if they are not available, substitute fantasy or masturbation. A useful critique of these studies can be found in Harper and Bain (1990). It is easy to see that this may be the basis of some men's excuse that their sex drive is uncontrollable and that they have to find expression for it with children if women or adult men are not available.

Psychodynamic and psychoanalytic theories

Psychodynamic and psychoanalytic theories are rooted in the work of Freud. They are based upon his views that unresolved sexual conflicts are at the root of all personality disorders. Either the child is seen to 'seduce' its father as a result of acting out 'oedipal desires', or in adult life sexual abuse is viewed as a result of an unsatisfactory resolution of the Oedipus complex in the individual. It should be noted that Freud developed the Electra and Oedipus complexes after the public outcry against his discovery in his clientele in Vienna that children were being sexually abused.

Thus Freud 'discovered' and then repressed knowledge of intra-familial incest. Further, his idea that incest is the boundary between stability and chaos has encouraged society to deny that incest exists on a large scale. However, it is also true to say that psychoanalytic theory has not minimised the trauma of incest, indeed Anna Freud has argued that:

Far from existing as a fantasy, incest is thus also a fact, more widespread among the population in certain periods than others. Where the chances of harming a child's normal developmental growth are concerned, it ranks higher than abandonment, neglect, physical maltreatment, or any other form of abuse. It would be a fatal mistake to under estimate either the importance or the frequency of its actual occurrence. (Freud, 1981, p.34)

Groth (1979) developed a theoretical model of the sex abuser based upon psychoanalytic understandings. He defined the sex offender as being emotionally deprived, often abused as a child and often with a 'controlling' personality. He distinguished between the 'fixated' and 'regressed' personality.

The fixated personality, due to abnormal psychological development, becomes sexually attracted primarily or exclusively to children. The regressed personality, on the other hand, is able to maintain adult sexual relationships but reverts to the sexual abuse of children as a response to high levels of stress. This model has been highly influential in the development of typologies of offenders. Criticism of this school of thought looks at its reliance upon the stories of offenders themselves in understanding their sexual preferences.

It can also be regarded as a partial explanation that ignores the complexities of sexually abusive behaviour and the context in which it occurs. Ryan and Lane (1991) have attempted to assimilate the distinctions in offender types into a more contemporary theoretical framework and Salter (1988) distinguishes between offenders with a 'deviant arousal pattern' and offenders who 'sexualise non-sexual problems'.

Psychoanalytic theory has been located by feminist writers as being conceived largely within a patriarchal set of beliefs and assumptions. In their critique Macleod and Saraga (1988) argue

Abuse is generally understood as the man's response to a childhood history, featuring acute anxiety about sexual inadequacy, fear of castration and rage at the 'mother'. This of course individualises the problem and takes for granted a particular construction of male-female relationships and masculine sexuality. It asks not questions about this association of powerlessness, violence and sexuality in male sexuality and none about the 'mother', and thus abandons men and abusers to a theory and practice that offer little hope of rescue from the idea of uncontrollable male sexuality and misogyny. (Macleod & Saraga, 1988, p.31)

In this way it can be argued that whilst offering an explanation for the phenomena of child sexual abuse, psychoanalytic theory serves to underpin the power dynamics of a patriarchal society and offers women and children little or no hope that child sexual abuse can be eradicated from our society.

For us, work with sexual abusers must acknowledge that sexual abuse is overwhelmingly perpetrated by men against women and children and is a function of male power in a society that is patriarchal: that is, primarily focused on men's needs to the detriment of women and children. Moreover, we argue that child sexual abuse and its close companion domestic violence will not be reduced until men honestly acknowledge the negative and abusive aspects of their power and work hard at redressing the power imbalance to develop a society that in itself is not a danger to women and children. Although we do recognise that women can be child sex abusers, they account for only a small percentage of the known perpetrators of child sexual abuse.

Family dysfunction theory

Family dysfunction theory, developed from family psychiatry in the 1940s, is the dominant orthodoxy amongst many professionals today. Abuse is described as being the property of the family system because 'normal' family boundaries, hierarchies and relationships have broken down. De Young (1982) describes these conditions as follows:

> ... the wife has become alienated for some reason; the father is too inhibited or moralistic to find sexual satisfaction outside the family, thus blocked gratification, he turns to his daughter as a substitute. (De Young, 1982)).

Gebhard et al (1965) argue that these circumstances develop during periods of marital stress. Macleod and Saraga (1988) have questioned many aspects of this theory, in particular its tendency to 'mother blaming' and its references to 'abusing parents' when almost all sexual abusers are men. Family dysfunction theory is a branch of systems theory which increasingly seems unsophisticated in its conception of family members' roles and power relations and the nature of sexuality.

Nonetheless, this theory does acknowledge that child sexual abuse is far more common than is generally believed by professionals and society as a whole. The belief that children fantasise about abuse is rejected (the latest manifestation of this belief being False Memory Syndrome theory). Dysfunction theories state firmly that the victim is not to blame and that the abuser alone is responsible for the act of abuse, even though blurring of family boundaries is seen as a causal factor. In effect, if the family was not dysfunctional, then the abuse would not have taken place! Further, such theories neither account for children abused outside the family, (by friends, relatives etc) nor acknowledge that intrafamilial abuse is not restricted to father/daughter incest.

The seminal work of this approach is *The Multi-professional Handbook of Child Sexual Abuse* by Tilman Furniss (1991), which brought together published and unpublished work from the previous 15 years. In it, Furniss makes a distinction between two sorts of family: conflict avoiding and conflict regulating. He argues that child sexual abuse serves as a function of either avoiding or regulating conflict between parents. The argument pivots around maternal behaviour which is seen to follow a distinct pattern in each type of family.

The first kind of maternal behaviour that is looked at in this model is what is termed Conflict Avoiding. This is described well in the following quote from Porter:

> *The mother sets the rules for emotional relationships and for the way emotional matters are talked about. (Porter, 1984, p. 12)*

The mother is seen as emotionally distant from the daughter who is used by the father to satisfy his 'depth needs for care, warmth and sex' which are not being met by the mother. If the daughter tells the mother about the abuse in this scenario, it is argued that the disclosure will be dismissed. The damage of abuse is compounded by perceived lack of caring from the mother. Thus the daughter is doubly abused.

In the second type of family dynamic, Conflict Regulating, the mother is an equal with the children and the daughter takes on a parental role with each of the parents.

> *The mother is deficient in practical as well as emotional support for the children. She becomes their 'pseudo equal'. (Porter, 1984, p. 12)*

In this kind of family it is said that the girl who is being abused may have adopted the role of mother to her own parents. Conflict and even violence between the parents is overt, and the child is 'sacrificed' to regulate the conflict and avoid family breakdown.

In both types of family the child sexual abuse is seen as a symptom of what is wrong in a family or even a 'solution' to the dysfunction. The problem to be addressed is therefore not the sexual abuse of the child, but the underlying dysfunction. In analysis, almost every family is seen to have broken down because of some lack in the mother. As Macleod and Saraga (1988) point out, there is an unwritten assumption here that families are functional when men's' needs are met. The message, at a simplistic level, is that if women are not sexually compliant to their men they cause men to sexually abuse children. Often the stories of men who perpetrate sexual abuse against children fit into this assumption; the wife was not interested or frigid so they turned to the daughter. There can also be, in conjunction with this, a feeling of right of ownership of the daughter. Taken together these two beliefs allow a cognitive distortion in the perpetrator which gives permission for him to have sex with his child or stepchild, and not see this as an abusive action but as a 'right'.

Critiques of this model (Herman, 1981; Nelson, 1987; Bagley & King, 1991) suggest that an approach that supports non-abusing carers might be more effective in promoting the long-term well-being of children. If this is promoted, then children may grow up to value caring and seek to replicate that, rather than the destructive types of power employed by abusing fathers in a family relationship.

Moreover, in this model, there is no discussion on the role of the father. It seems to be implicit that men's needs are paramount, a replay of old biological models of sexuality which says that the male sex drive is uncontrollable and if not released in women, requires the use of children as a substitute. This argument does two things. It does a great disservice to the majority of men who do not sexually abuse children and also places women's sexuality as being contingent upon men's and not an entity in its own right. Women are seen as part of the system, however they are a 'special' part, because if they fail in their role children are at risk. Therefore:

It is up to women not only to nurture and care for their men adequately, and to control their own desires, but also to control men's sexuality. Since men are unable to control themselves, and are seen as being 'addicted', there is always the danger that it will happen again. Bentovim and others argue that children can be safe in the family only if their mothers can protect them. (Macleod and Saraga, 1988, p.34)

Such views are often unwittingly stated in case conferences where woman are frequently judged to have 'failed to protect'. Once again the abusing male partner's responsibility for the damage caused to a child is reduced and modified.

Nevertheless this approach argues persuasively that blame and responsibility be taken away from individuals and placed in the family system, where everyone is a victim of a family dysfunction. If blame is removed, it is argued, then we can move away from a punitive model to a treatment or therapeutic model since:

the emphasis in punishing the perpetrator which was prevalent in the English approach and in the media meant that the victim would conceal the problem and make it harder to identify. (Bentovim quoted in the Guardian *8th September 1987).*

This argument fails to see that what it is actually expounding is removing responsibility from the male perpetrator and putting it on the mother. In its theoretical base this view gives little help in understanding why some men choose to sexually abuse children and why some women who were abused themselves enter into relationships in which their own children are abused. Bentovim states:

Some families seem to recreate the pattern of relationships that occurred in their family of origin, focusing around stressful events and relationships. So at its simplest fathers abuse as their fathers abuse, daughters are abused as their mothers were. (Porter, 1984, p.45).

There are two problems with this view. Firstly, given the known frequency of child abuse, if all men who abuse had been abused themselves it would mean a huge amount of undisclosed abuse of boys. However, research currently tells us that there are many more men who abuse than were abused. In this respect, Groth (1979) put forward the argument that it is harder for boys to disclose than girls, particularly in late adolescence. Secondly, research indicates high levels of abuse of girls and a low incidence of child sexual abuse by women.

It would seem that family systems theory which sees sexual abuse as a symptom of family dysfunction, and puts both the blame for the abuse and responsibilities for reforming the family on women, offers little hope to victims in the terms of their perpetrators accepting responsibility and stopping their behaviour.

It is interesting to note here that the NSPCC Child and Family centre in Bedminster in Bristol have been piloting a scheme for working with families where responsibility for the abuse is denied and there is not enough evidence to take the alleged abuser to court. We have some reservations about this approach as this may compound the mind set that sexual abuse is a symptom of a dysfunctional family and that the family per se needs to change their behaviour and not the perpetrator who is the person who is damaging the family. It is our opinion that a shift away from the 'mother blaming' that is endemic within family therapy approaches to child sexual abuse is essential if men are to take responsibility for their actions, and society is to be better protected.

The view that women have to keep children safe from men has further consequences. After family therapy male perpetrators can be allowed back into a family provided that the women is seen as 'strong' enough and therefore able to protect her children. The strength of this approach is that it offers a way of treating and helping perpetrators and their families that does not stigmatise the perpetrator and enables families to stay together if they so wish.

This is a realistic option for some families after disclosure in that the victim will want the abuse to stop and at the same time may want the family to stay together. For some victims criminal proceedings against their abuser is not what they want, and can add to their feelings of guilt and responsibility. At the same time seeing the abuser prosecuted, stand trial and be convicted may be important in the journey from victim to survivor to thrivor for some. We cannot homogenise the feelings of victims as all will be different and need a variety of inputs from the helping professions and non-abusing family and friends. Victims can and do recover from all kinds of abuse and need to hear the message very clearly that recovery is possible and that negative long term effects need not be the future outcome.

Later expositions of the theory, for example Driver and Droison (1989), have stated that the dysfunctional elements of the family are now more likely to be seen as a result of abuse rather than its cause. Further, workers within family systems theory have begun to differentiate between physical abuse and child sexual abuse. (Crittendon, 1988; Stratton, 1991; Hanks, 1993).

More recent developments by De Shazer (1984, 1989) access constructivist ideas. Here the focus is on how individuals construct a 'reality' of life experiences or events. An individual is seen to perceive events through their own filter and then construct a belief about what happened. McCluskey and Bingley Miller (1995) have combined focal family therapy and theme-focused family therapy in order to allow adults to re-edit the past and allow children to look at their concerns and feelings arising from their experience of being in a dysfunctional family system. The work at the NSPCC project at Bedminster in its second stage, engages families in a hypothetical exercise which enables them to look at how they and others in the family may be experiencing abuse. (Essex, Gumbleton & Lugar, 1996).

Behavioural theories

Contemporary behavioural explanations for child sexual abuse focus more specifically upon the perpetrator. Sexual offending is seen as the result of 'faulty' learning during an individual's psycho-sexual development; in effect a conditioning process which associates certain stimuli with particular responses. Accordingly, sexual abuse is caused when perpetrators 'pair' the bodies of children with sexual arousal and then act upon these responses. Cook and Howells (1981) describe this process as 'attributional error'. Children elicit strong emotional feelings in adults and responses should be parental, protective and affectionate. However, for perpetrators, these messages are incorrectly understood and interpreted sexually, which can impute a sexual, component to the ordinary behaviour of children.

Wolf (1984) writes that early physical, emotional or sexual abuse leads to personality types predisposed to deviant sexual interests and arousal. If an adult with these experiences has 'poor impulse control' they are then:

Unable to defer gratification or tolerate frustration until a socially suitable situation is available. (Finklehor, 1986)

Sex offenders within this theoretical framework are seen as having low self esteem, feelings of inadequacy and powerlessness. This leads to an inability to develop adult to adult relationships and results in the offender withdrawing into deviant sexual fantasies that are re-inforced by masturbation. If the fantasy fails to satisfy the man and he crosses the boundary from the acting out of an illegal fantasy to the actual abuse of a child, his feelings of inadequacy and low self-esteem will be further re-inforced thus encouraging the man to repeat his cycle of abuse.

Marshall (1996) links low self-esteem to faulty attachments in childhood. Within the Toronto treatment programme considerable attention is paid to methods of re-parenting, developing social skills and thus a healthy self-esteem. For Marshall this is the key to stopping offending.

The notion that sexually abusive behaviour towards children is based upon a repetitive and self re-enforcing pattern of behaviour is widely accepted by practitioners and is also underpinned by research evidence (see Abel et al, 1985).

Nevertheless, the implied causal relationship between childhood experiences, faulty learning and adult sexual offending is problematic. For example, we know that most abused children do not become perpetrators and that not all perpetrators have themselves suffered sexual abuse. Whilst these theories draw attention to the importance of childhood learning for adult development, they can, on the other hand, serve to detract from the responsibility of the adult abuser. No amount of abuse suffered as a child can give an adult permission to go on and themselves abuse children, and therefore add to the accumulation of victim pain.

Both sociological and feminist theory reject psychological contributions to the field of child sexual abuse because they do not address the social, political and economic context of all human action. Sociological theories on child sexual abuse focus on the diversity of sexual experiences and practices. It is argued that 'deviant' behaviour is constructed from and defined by 'social norms'. Child sexual abuse is therefore something which is defined and judged against other forms of sexual behaviour in social terms, rather than being viewed as an individual 'sickness' or 'disease'. Plummer (1981) attempts to locate child sexual abuse as one type of sexual behaviour amongst many others which cut through the social strata of age, gender, sex and class. It is helpful, therefore, to locate the sexual abuse of women and children on a continuum of general male sexual behaviour.

Feminist theory

Feminist theory on child sexual abuse explains the phenomenon as a logical extension of the power imbalance between men, women and children within a patriarchal society. Men maintain control over the lives of women in a patriarchal society because of structural inequalities. Gocke (1991) sees this as being in order for men to be serviced domestically, economically, socially and sexually. What we have therefore is:

... a culture that assumes dominance of men over women and children gives permission for men to sexually abuse. (Rush, 1990)

These assumptions are seen to permeate society at every level. These cultural norms are assimilated as part of children's socialisation process. Male children are socialised to believe that they are the natural initiators and 'aggressors' in sexual encounters. Men's 'entitlement' to women is sustained by media images of male/female relationships, and pornography, which perpetuates the myth of women as available and as sex objects. Driver and Droisen (1989) use this perspective to explain the dynamics of child sexual abuse. Male perpetrators are seen as:

Acting within the mainstream of sexual behaviour which sees women as sexual commodities and believes men have the right to use and abuse these commodities however and wherever they can. (Driver & Droison, 1989)

While these inequalities within power relations exist, women and children are consigned to subordinate roles and sexual abuse of children is

a further extension of non-consensual relationships between peers. (Hooper, 1991)

Child sexual abuse can thus be seen as one spectrum of male violence against women and children. Feminist theory asks the question why male rage is turned on women and children and finds the answers in terms of the dominant ideologies of sexism and racism within our society.

Not only do these structural inequalities provide the 'permission' for men to abuse their power over women and children, society is so male orientated that women are often blamed for the sexual abuse of children. To build on a point stated earlier by Dietz and Craft (1980) society can be seen as 'fuelling women blame' by accusing them of failing in, firstly, their sexual duties to their partners, and then failing to protect their children when they are abused because they have failed to meet the needs of their men. Driver and Droisen argue that psychiatric theories on child sexual abuse perpetuate these misconceptions:

By ignoring the fathers desire and, more importantly, his social power to act upon it, the psychiatric literature effectively shifts blame from the perpetrator to the survivors. (Driver & Droisen, 1989)

Frosch argues further:

There are important and difficult questions concerning the processes whereby most men learn not to abuse children - processes presumably connected with the quality of their relationships in early life, internalisation of moral constraints, and the development of capacities to form positive sexual and emotional relationships with adults. But if there are systemic factors that make men more likely to sexually abuse children, then these factors will be present more or less strongly in all men. (Frosh, 1987, p.335)

All men therefore should be prepared to look at the problems inherent in masculine socialisation which encourages men to express anger; and the sexualisation of male emotion which results in the sexualisation of rage and anger.

This anger has been defined in terms of the 'disease model' and this, according to Jeffreys (1985) helps to marginalise the responsibility that patriarchy generally and male perpetrators specifically must take for child sexual abuse. Instead blame is apportioned to a few very different 'exceptional' or 'sick' individuals. Langan and Day (1992) see this view of sex offenders being seen as 'mad rather than bad" as a way of absolving individuals and society from the responsibility for child sexual abuse.

The feminist critique of family systems theory has helped to highlight the propensity for 'mother blaming' in most other theoretical perspectives. Waterhouse stated:

Rather than recognising the potential women have for helping their children overcome the effects of abuse, there is evidence that social workers tend to hold onto pre-conceived notions that blame mothers for the abuse. (Waterhouse, 1993)

Waterhouse has argued that there is research evidence that mothers play a crucial role in the recovery of sexually abused children and indeed act protectively in the majority of cases (see: Hooper, 1992; Winters, 1990). These studies place the responsibility for the abuse with the perpetrator rather than the family as a whole. Hopefully the will begin to lead to a change in emphasis, so that the perpetrator is removed from the home in the cases of intra-familial abuse, not the child. Removing an abused child can often compound the abuse already suffered. If possible a child should remain at home with multi-agency support.

At present, feminist theory, is no more able than any other theory to explain why some men sexually abuse children, while most do not. Current research at Great Ormond Street is beginning to consider this issue. In our view, answers to this question would be of great value. As the reasons why perpetrators abuse seem so complex, knowing why people do not abuse may help us in the fight to prevent damage and injury to children in the future.

Psychological/socio-cultural theories

Psychological/Socio-cultural theories of child sexual abuse adopt a 'holistic' view of sexual offending which takes into account the social and cultural factors which impinge upon behaviour. These theories locate the responsibility for abuse with the perpetrators, and have built upon earlier behaviourist approaches to provide a cognitive behavioural view of sexual offending which is also integrated within a societal framework. Finkelhor (1986) has been dominant in this field and criticises 'single factor theories' for their inadequacies in explaining the diversity and complexity of child sexual abuse. He offers an alternative model, arguing that there are four preconditions that must be met by a potential perpetrator before a child can be sexually abused:

1. There must be motivation to sexually abuse
2. Internal inhibitions not to abuse must be overcome.
3. External inhibitors must be overcome (e.g. manipulating the environment).
4. The victims resistance must be overcome.

He argues that his work draws the deficiencies of so-called linear theories into a more manageable framework:

It encourages an appropriately complex view of the situation and at the same time gives some order to the confusing array of theories that have been proposed. (Finkelhor, 1986)

This approach draws from the psychological theories of Groth (1979) and the behavioural models of Wolf (1984) and brings them together within a sociological framework. Both situational and environmental influences on the abusers' behaviour are crucial to this approach. It is seen as vital that workers understand the interaction between the internal world of an individual (including the cognitive distortions he carries) and the external social world in which he operates.

The component parts of this approach can be looked at in the following ways:

1. Men are socialised to prefer partners who are younger, smaller,

innocent, vulnerable and powerless. In effect the woman is seen as childlike. Therefore if, for whatever reason, adults are not available as sexual partners men will be sexually attracted to children.

2. Men are expected to initiate sexual encounters, they have to overcome resistance and sometimes view resistance as a cover for desire - 'No' really means 'Yes'.

3. Men appear to be more promiscuous than women - this is seen as biological (Symons, 1979).

4. Men seemed to be more easily aroused than women by pornography, that is stimuli divorced from the context of a relationship. This may be because men react to visual stimulus more readily than women.

5. Men sexualise the expression of emotion. They find it difficult to distinguish situations of affection and intimacy (say within a family) which do not involve sex from those that properly do. Men are likely to assign all affectionate contacts as sexual and become aroused.

6. Men view lack of sexual opportunities in a way that affects their self-esteem. Therefore if no adult opportunities for sexual expression exist they may turn to children in order to fulfil their sexual desire and therefore maintain their sense of self esteem.

7. Sexual contact with children appears to be condoned by male sub culture. Rush (1980) has documented how sexual involvement between men and children has been accepted or encouraged throughout western history.

Fuller in 1989 provides an illustration of how these interactive processes work:

Pre-requisites	Contributing Factors	Outcome
Sexual attraction to Children	Cultural	Child Sexual Abuse
	Environmental	
Willingness to act on feelings of sexual attraction to children	Individual	
	Family	

In more recent years theories which rest within this paradigm have been developed which regard sexual abuse against children as analogous to addictive behaviour, which like alcohol addiction can be controlled but not 'cured' (Salter, 1988; Fuller, 1989 ; Ryan & Lane, 1991; Hooper, 1992; Morrison et al, 1995). Unlike those who have attempted to find a causal explanation and therefore a cure for child sexual abuse, eclectic theorists have developed programmes of treatment based upon cognitive-behavioural models to help perpetrators control their behaviour. Thus Wolfs' (1984) cycle of abuse has been developed together with work by Prochaska and Diclementi (1982) on the addiction cycle, which have been linked with Millers' (1982) motivational interviewing techniques to provide a model of working with men who sexually abuse children.

As such child sexual abuse is in many ways much closer to drug and alcohol addiction than to 'normal' physical abuse and neglect. (King & Travell, 1992)

In the UK, the Gracewell Clinic (now the Lucy Faithful Foundation) established a residential facility to deliver a cognitive-behaviourist programme based upon the Minnesota model from America developed in the early 1980s. The Probation Service and other agencies have used a similar approach to set up community based programmes across the country.

Waterhouse states that the key to this approach is the

degree of culpability and responsibility accorded and accepted by sexual offenders.

The offender is encouraged to own the abuse and is encouraged to work through denial, minimisation and rationalisation in order to accept responsibility. Salter (1988) summarises the process as follows:

1. To reduce risk the perpetrator must understand his motivation and stimuli which contribute to his offending.
2. Structural patterns are highlighted.
3. Perceptions, attitudes and therefore actions can be changed.
4. Self monitoring and 'control' can then take place.

Amongst practitioners in particular, it is recognised that these eclectic theories on child sexual abuse have had a major contribution towards the development of strategies in helping offenders control their behaviour.

There is progress towards a general consensus (of research) that simplistic, biological, medical and political or cultural accounts have little to offer which is of direct, practical assistance to those working with the problem of sexually abusive behaviour. Fewer professionals now talk in terms of cause and effect. (Waterhouse, 1993)

Baker and Morgan (1993) describe this multi-faceted approach as being data driven. The STEP report which conducted an evaluation study of seven such programmes concluded that they were able, in some cases, to bring about change in men who sexually abuse children. To succeed, work with the more 'serious' offenders must not only be intensive but also long term. Rapists should not be treated with child sex abusers as the programmes for the former have little impact on the latter (Marshall & Barbaree, 1990).

Discussion

Despite their power and potential, the eclectic theories do not address the socio-political and economic reality within which the men who sexually abuse operate. Child sexual abuse and the consequential victimisation of children continues. Only a small percentage of men who abuse are suitable for treatment programmes and many who are suitable do not get the opportunity because of limitation on places or the practice of only offering places to convicted abusers or those with a 'finding of fact'. In prison in England, the sentence has to be longer than 4 years for a convicted abuser to be given an automatic place on the Sexual Offenders Treatment Programme.

Furthermore the treatment programmes themselves are not able to address the need for fundamental changes within society. The funding decisions are, of course, made within a society that continues to discriminate against women and children.

Research into child sexual abuse is also located within this society which does not usually address the deep rooted problems of sexism and racism within itself.

Prevention is normally based upon an understanding of the cause. The strategy is to intervene in the causal chain to avoid the unwanted outcome. It is notoriously difficult to unravel the causal pathways of human social behaviour. This is even more complex when the behaviour in question, is not open to simple behavioural definition and measurement. (Waterhouse, 1993)

The relationship between cause and effect in the social sciences is difficult to establish, and is therefore open to varied interpretation. Parton (1991) believes that research in social work can be used to prove or disprove anything. In the study of perpetrators of child sexual abuse those difficulties mean that research must be treated with caution.

The reason for caution lies in the fact that the only the perpetrators could answer the question why some men abuse children—assuming that they know themselves and that their perceptions are located within reality itself. Child sexual abuse is in itself an emotive subject which is difficult to discuss in an open forum within wider society.

Research focused upon offenders provides us with validity problems in terms of the distorted thinking, rationalisation and minimisation that is a common feature amongst offenders. For men in treatment, or taking part in research, there are implications for honesty in that the threat of possible prosecution that accompanies full disclosure can skew the reliability of accounts given by perpetrators. (Salter, 1988)

Salter (1997) argued that unless one has access to a sophisticated polygraph (lie detector) test, perpetrators would not tell the truth about the number and seriousness of the offences that they have carried out. This has implications for the quality of information that we have from perpetrators about reasons for the perpetration of child sexual abuse.

The sampling of offenders is also problematic. Waterhouse has argued that the samples are often small scale and focus on prison or clinical populations who are in or have finished treatment programmes. Small scale samples cannot be regarded as being representative of the population of men who sexually abuse children, as they contain only those men who have been caught and either have admitted the abuse or have been found guilty. Also the very process of treatment may enable men to give researchers the answers they feel are 'right' and not necessarily 'true' for them. This maybe particularly pertinent if they are working towards re-integration with the family or some other 'reward'.

Furthermore studies have tended to focus on long term offenders and this has led to the development of the 'assumptive stance'. This means that therapists invariably assume that men have committed more offences than they have admitted or been caught for. Abel et al's (1986) study of a New York institute of psychiatric medicine showed that each offender had had an average of 75 victims before being caught. Ray Wyre has stated that in his work he has never met a first time offender. This can lead to the assumption that those men in treatment who do not confess to more offences are in denial and may be unsuitable for treatment. While it is accepted that some men will have many offences because of the addictive nature of child sexual abuse it must be equally true that there can be a continuum with first time and occasional offenders at one end, and, at the other, men with multiple offence careers. Each man's pattern is different: a man who takes years to groom his victim and the environment may have less victims than the opportunist offender who attacks strangers.

Finklehor (1986) argues that the characteristics of sex offenders drawn from research studies are common to those cases that the research world knows about. By definition these do not include those men who have not been caught or have not come forward voluntarily for treatment.

Fuller puts forward the view that:

A review of the literature on sexual abuse reveals a lack of appreciation of the variability in cases, and the fact that different types of cases require different intervention approaches. (Fuller, 1989)

That sexual abuse is itself defined in a multiplicity of ways within research studies makes it difficult to compare the results and conclusions reached. What is clear is that research in the field has produced very different views of child sexual abuse and the perpetrators of said abuse.

Hudson (1992) argues that there is a mystique that has built up around working with perpetrators which makes social workers in the field feel insecure about their abilities and skills. Giller et al (1992) argued that research is an under-used tool in child protection decision making. If this is the case the development of knowledge about the men who commit child sexual abuse should be available to social workers in a format that is accessible and actually helps contribute to their ability to work with the wider issues of child protection so that work with victims and perpetrators can be undertaken in an integrated way.

Bateson's (1972, 1980) notions of context and restraint as developed by White (1984, 1986a, 1986b) are particularly useful in explaining abusive behaviour. Jenkins (1990) has taken these ideas and produced an innovative treatment programme based on his theoretical perspective.

Abuse perpetrators can be seen to hold values and beliefs which act as restraints to the acceptance of responsibility for abusive actions and the development of sensitive and respectful relationships with others. These restraints are reflected in the ways that abusive males construct explanations for their abusive actions and blue prints for relating to others. Restraints are best understood by examining them in the context in which they have been developed and maintained. (Jenkins, 1990, p.14)

Conclusion

The notion that sexual abusers can take responsibility for and therefore control their abusive behaviour, which is a central tenet of Jenkins work is co-terminous with the feminist perspective that men have to take responsibility, firstly for their abusive behaviours, and secondly for a male orientated society that allows the ongoing abuse of women and children. Change has to take place within individual men and society as a whole if we are going to build a society that is safer for ensuing generations. As workers we can contribute to the individual changes that perpetrators need to make to prevent more children becoming victims.

Workers in the field need, therefore, to understand the internal world of the perpetrator of child sex abuse. In order to be able to abuse a child the perpetrator must first construct a belief system that allows the overriding of internal and external social, moral and legal norms. This is a difficult and often painful world for the worker to enter. However the theories and techniques explained in this book can help the worker order the chaos and the often seemingly arbitrary nature of child sex abuse. Understanding how perpetrators work, good support systems and supervision are essential to work in this area. The next chapter will build on the theoretical perspectives outlined here in order to increase understanding about how child sex abusers operate and the knowledge that we need to bring about change and control.

Chapter 2

How perpetrators abuse

MOST SEX abusers operate in a planned and premeditated way, and this planning is an important facet of the behaviour of all sexual abusers. It allows them to gain positions of trust within families, communities and organisations. Some may plan the abuse over years, gradually manoeuvring themselves into position to act out their fantasies on their victims – for some it may take only a matter of hours and minutes rather than years.

In choosing their victims abusers often target vulnerable women who are not coping with their family responsibilities. The abuser may becomes a friend to the parents and through them the children. The potential abuser may even move in, either as a friend of a two parent family or by seduction of a lone mother. Home life may then improve through their provision of support, treats for the children, baby-sitting to allow the parents or parent time off and their monetary contribution.

Abusers are often poor at developing mature, reciprocal, close emotional relationships with adults. As we have seen they can suffer from low self esteem and have a poor self image, and so may attempt to increase their feelings of self worth by gaining power over more vulnerable people. Finkelhor (1984) states that motivation for offending by a potential perpetrator is a necessary predisposing factor within the personality of the offender, for the abuse to occur. The motivation may be sourced to earlier life experiences or to something in the present. An example of the latter might be family friend of 25 years who abuses a 10 year old friend of his daughter and cites his recent impotence with his wife and her affair as contributing factors.

Perpetrators can form strong emotional links with their victims as they groom or manipulate both the environment and them. In many ways it could be argued that incidents of sexual abuse are part of a wider abusive relationship into which victims are gradually drawn through attention, treats and excitement. As this process develops children are likely to find it ever more difficult to resist the sexualisation of the relationship. Hence a frequent consequence is that children feel a degree of responsibility for the subsequent abuse and in retrospect may berate themselves for not preventing it. The first duty of the therapist is to work towards removing any sense of responsibility on the part of the victim. This is imperative if the victim is to move through the stages of victim-survivor-thrivor. Briere states (NOTA conference, 1998) that there is a higher risk of a female child abuse victim being raped in later life if they have not received adequate help post trauma.

The children perceived to be the most vulnerable will be targeted whether inside or outside the family (as previously discussed, most abuse takes place within the family). A 54 year old abuser, with hundreds of abusive acts for which he had not been caught, stated to Lynda that, if she placed 1,000 children in a room, it would take him about five minutes to spot his victim, and another five to isolate the child and perpetrate the abuse.

The abusive acts usually only take place if the abuser believes that they will not be found out, and the abuser will work hard to reduce the risk of this happening. Following an abusive act it is not uncommon for a perpetrator to remind a victim that they are also responsible for what has happened and that telling someone is likely to have negative consequences for both of them. Perpetrators can and will resort to violence if their seduction skills fail. In extreme situations, panic can lead abusers to kill victims to prevent discovery.

The commission of sexually abusive behaviour is a complex matter and as stated earlier there are two basic theoretical models that can help the worker beginning in this field. We will look first at Finkelhor's four stages or pre-conditions model in detail, and then move on to the sexual assault cycle developed originally by Wolf and adapted by many workers in the field.

Finkelhor's four stage model

Finkelhor's (1984) four pre-conditions model gives us a useful explanation of the process that perpetrators follow in order to sexually abuse children. Its also useful in helping to develop external controls for perpetrators which will be explored later. The first stage or step is:

Step 1: Motivation to sexually abuse

Fairly obviously there must be a degree of sexual arousal to a child or children if abuse is to take place. As previously discussed the origins of this may be 'way back when' in a perpetrator's life or may be more recent.

One client with whom Lynda worked was at this stage when he referred himself to her. He had been systematically abused as a child, both physically and sexually, by his stepfather. He had also been required to abuse his sisters whilst his parents looked on, and watch films made of this, as well as other pornography showing children with adults and occasionally animals. He had disclosed as an adult and his stepfather had been convicted and given a long sentence. A year after the conviction of his stepfather the client was getting off a bus that was carrying young school children found himself fantasising about sex with a child of 7 or 8. Despite having had some therapy he had not been prepared for this, and was very frightened. The physical desire to abuse was very strong. He called for help because he did not want to inflict the pain on children that he had suffered.

The motivation not to abuse was for this client greater, at this point, than the motivation to abuse. For perpetrators who go on to abuse this is clearly not the case. They make a decision to allow sexual desire or the need for power to override notions of morality and law. Typically they may fuel the fantasies that they are having about children by excessive masturbation, which can take place up to 20 times per day.

If the worker and the perpetrator can understand the stimulus that sets off the desire to abuse, then control strategies can be developed to enable the perpetrator to recognise triggers and to control fantasy in order to avoid moving on to the next stage in the process of abusing and harming children. For example, the perpetrator who was able to work out in therapy that he abused 11 to 12 year old fair haired boys only in woods was able to begin to be safe by avoiding woods and of course other secluded places where children play. By giving this information to the police he was able to have a further external safeguard, as he knew he would be a prime suspect if any sexual offences against children were reported in those areas.

Step 2: Overcoming internal inhibitors

Internal inhibitors are built around notions of conscience, morality and fear of the law. Each person's world view will differ in the importance accorded to these factors. However for most people one or a combination of these is enough to prevent offending of any sort. There are people who have illegal sexual fantasies who do not act them out and harm children. We do not know the extent of these types of sexual fantasy within the non-offending population, owing to the obvious difficulties in researching this topic. Nancy Friday (1973) did some qualitative research in the population at large, some of the results of which can be looked at in *My Secret Garden*. Workers in the field who regularly have to take perpetrators through their fantasies are, understandably, very reticent about disclosing their own. How much more difficult must it be for the ordinary person to disclose fantasies which are about having sexual activity with children? Research with those people who have, but do not act on, illegal fantasies would be helpful in informing the work that we do with those people who have acted on such fantasies.

Child sex abusers who cross this boundary develop an array of techniques to allow them to ignore the moral and legal imperative not to harm. The child's behaviour is often assigned causal power over sexual arousal and the sexual desire imputed to the child, rather than the perpetrator accepting that the problem was his inappropriate reaction to normal non-sexual behaviour on the part of the child. Abusers readily excuse or justify their behaviour. For example: 'I did not hurt her/him.'; 'S/he seduced me' (the three year old child came down stairs in nightclothes to sit on the perpetrators knee and thus 'caused' an erection).

Some perpetrators use disinhibitors such as drugs and alcohol and then blame this for their sexual abuse of a child. This distorted thinking is relatively easy to tackle as, if there was any truth in this there would be a direct link with alcohol or drug consumption and child sexual abuse. Drink and drugs do not cause sexual abuse, but they may serve to act as disinhibitors to allow the perpetrator to carry out action rooted in an existing sexual attraction to children.

Other ways of overcoming internal inhibitions are activities that reinforce beliefs that women and children are sex objects that somehow 'belong' to men who are thus free to do as they would wish. Membership of a group that promotes pornography in all its forms can serve to incrementally desensitise those who have an existing proclivity to abuse children. If others do it, then this validates the expression of illegal and immoral desires. Thus sex with children becomes 'normalised'. Recently, the prison service has become aware of rings formed among schedule 1 sex offenders which carry on after release, and which have the function of sharing information about pornography and where to access it. Of course the internet has made this type of desensitisation easier and increased the difficulty of policing the providers of such material.

Step 3: Overcoming external inhibitors

Once the child sex abuser has moved through the process of the first two steps they must create a situation in which the abuse can take place. This means removing or getting around external inhibitors such as protective adults so that unimpeded access to a child can be achieved. Perpetrators use all sorts of techniques to do this, including baby-sitting and organising children's activities. As already noted abusers moving in with lone parent families can be viewed as grooming the environment in order to facilitate abuse. One perpetrator who targeted 6 year old girls baby-sat for a family from birth, becoming a loved and reliable member of the family who were unaware that he was planning a special birthday present for the child. On her 6th birthday he raped her.

Child care agencies and churches are only now waking up to the risks that their staff can pose to the children in their care. Parents, unless they know of a child abused in the family home, are still not aware of the risks 'friends' can pose. The media informs the public about notorious extra-familial abusers who are undoubtedly dangerous. However they omit to inform the public of the much greater risk of child sexual abuse by a relative or known person.

Step 4: overcoming the resistance of the victim(s)

At this stage, the perpetrator will overcome any resistance to abuse by the victim. This can be achieved in a myriad of ways. It may be done by sophisticated seduction techniques that require the perpetrator to change the victims view of 'normal' behaviour. Over time the victims resistance will be lowered by incrementally moving physical behaviour from safe touching to overtly sexual contact. The victim may be introduced to pornography, drugs and or alcohol. The victim may know that these activities are in some way wrong but may have a sense of culpability and guilt, thus becoming an accomplice in their own abuse.

For many younger children compliance with the wishes of a much larger and intrinsically more powerful adult is straightforward. Many parents and carers and teachers give clear messages to children that adults know better and that children should do what adults tell them to. Alongside this there is a general reluctance among many parents about speaking to children about sex and the risks of sexual abuse. One child Lynda worked with felt anger towards her mother because she did not give her any sex education. She maintains that if she had she would have known that the actions of her stepfather were wrong and would have disclosed immediately rather than have abuse inflicted upon her for some 14 months.

One perpetrator that Lynda was working with on an individual basis said that, for him as an extra-familial abuser, overcoming the victims reluctance was not a problem. By virtue of the fact that he had gone through the first three stages he found that he did not experience any resistance from the victim. Chillingly he said that by this stage he had to abuse and if he met any resistance he would have no compunction in using violence. He later went on to state that he had decided in prison that if he returned to his abusing career he would think about killing the victim rather than risk disclosure and prison again.

Finkelhor's multi-factor model enables workers (and abusers and non-abusing partners in 'treatment') to envisage the components involved in the sexual abuse of a child. It is an inclusive model in that insights from a variety of theoretical perspectives can be used and in that it underlines the complexity of the behaviour and the interrelationships between thoughts, feelings, fantasy, and actions.

For sexual abuse to occur something must be occurring in all four factors or stages - an insight that can be used to assess future risk and help inform the development of risk management strategies.

For the practitioner beginning this work, the theoretical construct of Wolf (1984) who developed the sexual assault cycle and the addiction cycle work of Prochaska and Diclimente (1992) are tools to be added to the work of Finkelhor just discussed. However before we examine these, I would like to look briefly at four factor framework that Finkelhor (1984) developed alongside his four factor model already discussed. This gives us a more complex understanding of his work. However the reader who feels that at this stage they may become confused with factors and steps, may look at this later when they feel more confident in dealing with the material.

Finkelhor's four factor framework

Factor 1 looks at the emotional congruence that child sex abusers have with children. It would appear that children represent non-threatening objects, weaker than the abuser. For the offender who has a history of abuse or of being exposed to domestic violence there is some evidence of working through childhood trauma by identifying with the victim and repeating the abuse the perpetrator suffered. The group member who abused 11 year old boys in wooded areas and parks was reliving his own gang rape at that age. Some victims of sexual abuse go on to abuse in this way, but not all. Statistics indicate that about 25% of child sex abusers have been victims. Research at Great Ormond Street has been looking at this question for several years with four groups of boys, trying to find the link that causes some victims to lack empathy for victims and go on and replicate the behaviour of their abusers.

Factor 2 looks at the development of sexual arousal to children in adults. There have been differences in the data for intra-familial abusers and those that offend outside the family, and also inconsistencies in intra-familial abusers. Abel et al (1981) found an increased arousal to children. However, a later study by Marshall et al (1986) found that the subjects had a decreased arousal to adults rather than an increased arousal to children.

Factor 3 looks at why some adults are unable to meet their sexual and emotional needs within consenting adult relationships as part of a wider social interaction. Finkelhor cites two types of blockage, situational and developmental. The latter involves an inability to relate to adults sexually and the existence of poor social skills. In the forme case, an adult relationship exists but there is no sexual activity. We are not sure how far this factor takes our understanding of abuse. Firstly, there must be a sexual attraction to children for abuse to take place. Secondly, there are very many men who are either socially inadequate and unable to develop adult sexual relationships and those who are in a relationship which for some reason was or is no longer sexual and yet do not abuse children. This view does little to explain the small percentage of female abusers.

Factor 4 looks at why the moral and socio-legal inhibitions within our societies that forbids sexual contact between adults and children do not operate in child sex abusers. Poor or nonexistent impulse control is discussed as is the role of alcohol and drugs as a disinhibitor. The motivation to abuse children and a sexual attraction to them must be present as a separate category alongside these explanations for without these, poor impulse control and alcohol etc. would lead to other behaviours, as can be evidenced in the non-abusing majority.

Finkelhor puts forward the idea of an 'incest avoidance mechanism'. Evidence shows that there is more abuse by stepfathers than biological fathers. Again the question of female child sexual abusers is not looked at.

Wolf (1984) produced a model for looking at the *process* that child sex abusers must go through in order to abuse. When working with child sex abusers either individually or in groups or undertaking a risk assessment it is imperative that the workers are able to deconstruct the actions of the perpetrator and gain an understanding of each one's triggers and grooming process. The time that it takes for a abuser to enter the cycle and commit the abuse plus the type of abuse that s/he is perpetrating will give an indication of the risk that is posed to children and determine the conclusions and recommendations in each case.

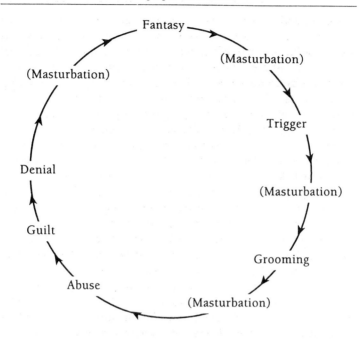

Figure 1. Abuse
Based on Wolf's cycle of offending (1984)
There is a more complex cycle based on Wolf's work in Morrison, T. Erooga, M. Becket, R.C. (eds) (1994) Sexual Offending Against Children. Assessment and Treatment of Male Abusers. London: Routledge.

Wolf's multi-factor model

For sexual abuse of children to take place the perpetrator has to be in and progressing around the above cycle. The details will be specific to a particular perpetrator. There may be many reasons why an individual might enter such a cycle. According to Wolf's multi-factor model there is a mixture of developmental, socio-cultural factors and situational factors. The developmental history of the perpetrator brings about a particular type of personality that is predisposed to deviant sexuality. For Wolf, sexual offenders have a particular type of personal history that engenders a sexual attraction to children. He talks about victimisation in early life together with a mixture of emotional and physical abuse. The physical abuse may be direct or indirect, through observing say a mother being the subject of violence. This abuse is often found with sexualisation and neglect within a dysfunctional family system, typified by low warmth, high criticism parenting. Recent research into domestic violence has found a link between this and intra-familial child sexual abuse. Goddard and Hillier (1993) found that domestic violence was a feature in 40% of child sexual abuse cases. In Farmer and Pollocks (1998) study of sexually abused and abusing children, 55% had lived in families where there was violence, mainly by the man to the women. Skuse (forthcoming) has found, in a small clinical sample, links between the sexual abuse of boys and domestic violence. There was a stronger correlation when the boys were both victims and perpetrators of sexual abuse.

Wolf argues that it is exposure to an abusive ethos rather than suffering abuse itself that is important in the development of a pattern of sexual behaviour harmful to others. For children exposed to abusive environments, where (usually) the male is the perpetrator of violence, a belief system is reinforced that males have power and can do as they like. This type of belief system serves to lessen inhibitions regarding the internal and external controls that feature in Finkelhor's model. (see factors 2 and 3)

For Wolf this type of personality development, which is typical of sexual offenders, whether against children or adults, encompasses character traits such as: egocentricity; poor self image; distorted thinking; obsessive thoughts and behaviour; and inability to make appropriate adult relationships leading to social alienation and a preoccupation with sex. This can lead to a process through which the sexual offender sexualises the behaviours of others, thus engendering the possibility of cognitive distortion of others' actions, and, in some cases, a belief that innocent actions by others are an invitation to sexual behaviour.

For many, escapism from their poor self esteem is found in sexual fantasy and excessive masturbation when feelings of control and power may be experienced. The more the level of arousal is increased the greater the likelihood of an offence taking place. Many perpetrators become drawn into the sexual assault cycle firstly because of poor self image and expectations of rejection from adult relationships. This can encourage withdrawal and the inability to be assertive which in turn can lead to compensatory fantasies and sexual escapism. To understand the masturbation cycle and how it reinforces sexual arousal that may lead to child sex abuse we need to look at the analogy of addiction and see it as a process rather than a single incident. The key component is the development of a pattern of sexual arousal to children. The fantasies are reinforced by regular masturbation and begin to dominate the fantasy life of the potential abuser. At this point the masturbation brings about the classical symptoms of addiction. These are:

- increasing preoccupation with the obtaining of sexual gratification;
- fantasies which become ever more detailed as the need for a greater 'kick' develops; *and*
- denial that this behaviour is or could be problematic.

The following shows the behaviour in diagrammatic form:

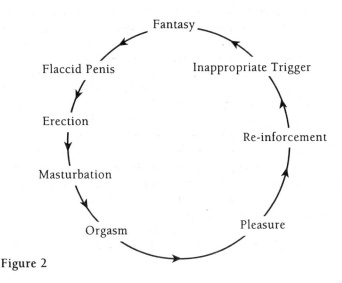

Figure 2

As discussed earlier, there is no necessary correlation between inappropriate sexual thoughts and fantasies and the perpetration of child sexual abuse. What is important and necessary for abuse to be committed is for the fantasies to trigger the perpetrator or potential perpetrator into the sexual assault cycle and for internal inhibitions against acting upon illegal fantasies to fail – in effect be overidden by the strength of the fantasy and the desire for a 'kick'

At the moment when a child triggers a sexual attraction in the perpetrator, the perpetrator begins the cycle that may lead to offending (see figure 1, p.31). The offender can feel powerful and in control in this situation. We will look in detail at how exactly a perpetrator can behave when in the sexual assault cycle.

Masturbating to images of children will put a potential perpetrator's internal inhibitors under pressure. This may be happening at the same time as s\he is undergoing external stressors, for example unemployment, debt or relationship failure. At this point drugs or alcohol may be used either consciously or unconsciously to disinhibit or reduce the internal inhibitors. At the same time, the potential perpetrator will employ cognitive distortions to minimise the compulsive/ addictive nature of sexual fantasies per se. Cognitive distortions are sophisticated in the sense that the person who is using them may not have fully conscious knowledge of this process.

If the process proceeds and the internal inhibitors are not restored then the masturbation and fantasy can become in effect a rehearsal for the real thing. It must be noted that one of the functions of rehearsal is to reduce anxiety and refine planning by acting out the intended abuse step by step.

At this point the potential abuser may begin to target a particular child, whether in the community or family, who may be vulnerable to his/her advances. This takes the typical form of befriending and creating a form of dependency. We have already seen how potent this can be in a one parent family. As contact with the child increases, detail will be added to the fantasy and masturbation of the perpetrator. At the same time cognitive distortions will be used in most cases to keep internal inhibitors reduced to a level that will allow an offence to take place. Some typical self-statements are: 'the child is provocative towards me', ' I am not doing any harm', ' the child is sexually interested in me', ' the child wants it'.

As the contact and thus the relationship with the child develops, the potential perpetrator will move on the next stage, grooming. This will include the child, the carers and the environment and situation in general. S/he will typically spend time with the child looking for opportunities to be alone and increase the level of intimacy with the child. Tools for this include: fun, affection (think of the effect of this on a child from a low warmth, high criticism dysfunctional family) presents etc all designed to engender an increasing closeness between the child and the potential perpetrator. As the above is happening, incremental physical contact will be introduced that will slowly become more intrusive and abusive. The victim is thus drawn into a distorted relationship, and thus their power to resist sexually abusive advances diminished. More cognitive distortions will be employed by the perpetrator to rationalise the developing abuses. For example ' I am only being affectionate', ' I will stop at stroking her leg' etc. As contact with the child increases and becomes more abusive the perpetrator will incorporate what is happening into more and more detailed sexual fantasies based on the developing situation. In this way the level of sexual arousal will gradually be increased.

As we said earlier, the grooming may take place quickly or may require a considerable period. The length of time that is spent on this part of the process is a crucial factor in the level of guilt experienced by the victim following the abuse and of their ability to keep safe subsequently. Similarly, and most importantly, this will also impact on the victim's ability to disclose directly.

The perpetrator is now involved in a spiral of increasing masturbation and sexual excitement fueled by inappropriate fantasy and the development of power in the relationship with the victim. Any internal inhibitors which existed before the process began are now reduced. S/he will now begin to look for the opportunity to offend. Perpetrators will not generally act unless they feel that the planning will ensure that the potential victim will cooperate and also will not tell. The perpetrator's judgement on this may be flawed by a number of factors including learning disability, mental illness, increasing sexual excitement and distorted thinking.

The commission of the abuse will, for many abusers, reinforce all the components of the sexual assault cycle. Fantasy will become more detailed and incorporate the overt incident of abuse within it and new ideas for disempowering the victim may be developed. For other abusers, the actuality of the act of abuse may not live up to the expectations generated by the preceding process.

Abusers who report significant sexual gratification from a first offence will often also report feelings of guilt and dysphoria in the period just after the abuse of the child. It is at this point they may worry about being caught and may try to bribe or threaten the victim in order to silence them. Some examples of this are 'if you tell, we will both be in trouble, I'll go to prison and you will go into care'. ' if mummy finds out she won't love you any more'. 'If you tell I will kill the dog/cat or the carer that is not abusing'.

Guilt may also cause the questioning of previous cognitive distortions, if this has been 'I will only rub her leg' and the abuse has consisted of touching the vagina or some form of oral sex, the distortions will have to change to encompass the act. For example 'I only did that because she encouraged me when I rubbed her leg'. Thus responsibility for the abuse is directed towards the victim.

The feeling of guilt together with worries about being caught may keep the perpetrator out of the cycle for a time; for some this may be weeks, months or years even, for others it may be five minutes, and may diminish in proportion to the risk of immediate discovery. However, if the perpetrator uses masturbation as a method of stress reduction it is likely that the return to illegal fantasy will be sooner than later. Return requires the rebuilding of the cognitive distortions and the reframing of the negative aspects of the offence. If the victim has not told anyone the perpetrator will be thinking things like 'I cannot have harmed her', ' I won't let myself go that far again'.

The stress felt from actually carrying out an act of sex abuse may now well be added to the original stressors that the perpetrator experienced when starting out around the assault cycle. This may ensure the continued use of drugs and alcohol if they were an original feature. This will contribute to the weakening of any resolve not to reoffend made in the initial aftermath of the first offence and of any feelings of guilt and revulsion with self that this can engender. Continued thinking about the offence will add to the original cognitive distortions which should be seen as a dynamic and continually evolving process enabling the perpetrator to continue to convince themself that the victim was not harmed. So the distortions may now well be of the following nature: 's/he has not told because they enjoyed it', 'there is a special kind of love between us'.

There is a risk then of the abuser moving around their cycle

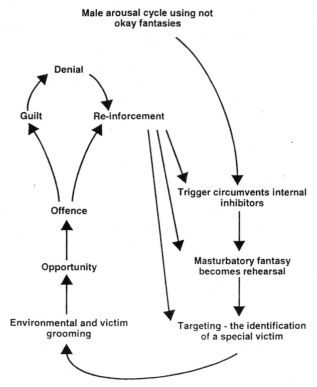

Male arousal cycle using not okay fantasies

Figure 3. Cycle of male sexual arousal, After Ryan et al, 1987

again and the more often this happens the more disempowered and isolated the victim feels. The second and subsequent offences may be more like masturbatory rehearsal than the first, providing more reinforcement if he/she is not caught again. And of course the more times a perpetrator gets away with an abusive act the less likely become feelings of guilt and the more likely that the abuse may become increasingly serious. Cognitive distortions continue to operate for example 'I am only fondling, not having intercourse', 'S/he likes having my penis in their mouth or s/he would say no'.

The male arousal cycle can be seen in the above diagram adapted from Ryan et al (1987)

For some offenders the time between the trigger and offending will be short whereas for others it can be considerable. Whatever the time, the successful execution of abuse will reinforce the beliefs in their power and ability to manipulate the environment and potential victims for their own use.

The quicker an individual gets around their particular cycle, the more dangerous they are as he/she has less opportunity to re-establish inhibitors. Those whose fantasies progress in seriousness over time also tend to present a high risk. This is because of the addictive nature of sexual abuse of any kind. The rehearsal or fantasy stage can become stale unless new activities are added at regular intervals. In this way the fantasy can become more serious over time to keep up the wanted level of stimulation. This, in turn, leads to more and more serious acts. There is a belief that an offender who does not perpetrate a 'contact' offence is less dangerous. What we know about many child sex abusers is that their offences progress in seriousness over time. This is partly to do with the reinforcement of getting away with an abusive act and also the need to keep their fantasies fresh and exciting. Repeating the same act over and over again eventually becomes boring, the escalation will also therefore depend on the individual's boredom threshold.

Conclusion

- For an abuser to offend there must be a sexual attraction to children. This may be obvious to the abuser, or repressed.
- The four preconditions must exist so that the abuser is not governed by the rules of social morality and the laws of society.
- The abuser must have access to victims and thereby be in a position to be triggered into the cycle of abuse.
- The abuser must be adept at cognitive distortions in order to minimise, if not entirely remove any guilt that they experience post abuse.
- The abuser must be adept at wearing a mask towards the outside world so that his internal world is hidden. In the case of abusers who work in tandem with others they may have less need of this strategy as they will spend considerable time with other abusers who accept their abusive behaviour.
- The abuser must be willing to inflict physical, psychological and emotional pain on their victims.

Chapter 3

How to work with perpetrators

WORKERS ENGAGE in work with perpetrators of child sex abuse for many reasons including:

- for social workers, assessing and managing risk to a family when a schedule 1 offender moves in or returns after a custodial sentence;
- risk assessments for Pre-Sentence Reports by probation officers; *and*
- therapeutic work with perpetrators by social workers, probation officers, housing workers and community psychiatric nurses.

All are concerned with protecting children and therefore helping to make society a safer place. Assessment of risk will be considered in the following chapters. Here we deal with the principles that should underpin all work with perpetrators whether they have been convicted in the criminal courts, have a finding of fact against them in the family court or are among those very few who have come forward on an informal basis in the hope of finding help.

The first tenet of working with perpetrators is to treat them with respect as many-faceted fellow human beings. This is not to condone the abusive behaviour, but to recognise that it is just one part of their make-up and does not mean that they are totally bad people. In many cases, the poor self esteem already identified as a likely contributory factor to abusing will have been exacerbated by the guilt of being caught and subjected to aggression and the contempt of others (who are likely to subscribe to the popular notion of sexual offenders as being monsters, perverts and animals to be vilified). Furthermore, those abusers who have been imprisoned will have experienced segregation for their own safety and real fear of violent retribution from other inmates For many the shaking of their hand by the worker may be the first non-abusive physical contact that they have experienced since sentencing or before. This may be an important factor in how effective the therapist or worker can make the therapeutic alliance.

The importance cannot therefore be underestimated of treating perpetrators with a sense of kindness and humanity, even though this can at times be difficult.

We will look elsewhere at the importance of good supervision and co-working relationships and the role that gender may play in this.

We need to look now to how we use the theories and concepts covered in chapters 1 and 2, in effect how we turn theory into practice in order to work with perpetrators of child sexual abuse.

Denial

Denial is a complex phenomena ranging from deliberate blatant lies to largely subconscious defensiveness. It is not a fixed state, rather part of a complex process, that can change as perpetrators retreat or move forward over time. Moving through denial is therefore not a linear progression and can be a complex interaction of circumstance and events.

Some may profess their innocence and make an issue about being 'found guilty' rather than 'pleading guilty'. Some may make partial acknowledgement of their abusive behaviour and some may be in complete denial. For many writers and commentators in this field, denial is seen as a negative reaction, and often at the assessment stage perpetrators are considered unsuitable for treatment programmes if this persists. However we feel that this is a negative view of what is essentially a psychological reaction to either initially admitting or being found guilty of crimes that most people find unspeakable and hard to comprehend. Denial is better understood as a function of psychological survival, which originated in negative distortions employed to allow offending to take place, and which will persist as long as the perpetrator feels the need to hide the true nature and impact of their actions both from themselves and the outside world.

Denial has become an important concept in understanding how sex offenders operate and respond to assessment and intervention. It is normally used as a general term to describe the array of rationalising cognitions or 'thinking errors' typically employed by sexual offenders to disinhibit themselves in the build-up to and the commission of offences. It can, therefore, be viewed as a functional component of the sexual assault cycle. Following disclosure of abuse, such a defence mechanism is often adapted and developed in an attempt to manipulate the dynamics, context and outcome of risk assessments. In many ways, this represents a continuation of the grooming process that was operating before and during offending. Recent work by Anna Salter (1998) has led her to produce training tapes, including 'Truth, Lies and Sex Offenders'. This shows how five convicted sex offenders convincingly employed denial, blatant lies and the doing of apparently good works to ensure that when they were accused of child sexual abuse the community did not believe the allegations.

As already stated denial is a complex phenomena:

- It can range from blatant lies to largely subconscious defensiveness.
- It is not a binary function but a spectrum of minimisations and rationalisations.
- It is not a fixed state, but part of a process and its manifestation may alter across location context and a time.

Anna Salter (1988) suggests a categorisation of denial which indicates the diversity of the rationalising cognitions that may be used:

Admission with justification

This may involve acknowledging that an offence has been committed but seeking to justify such behaviour. For example: 'she deserved it', 'she was provocative', 'I was educating her'. This can be connected with the 'philosophical' stance that sex with children is morally acceptable and that society's criminal isolation of such behaviour is erroneous.

Outright denial of the act

This often involves the collusion of others in order to provide an alibi. Attempts are frequently made to discredit the victims veracity and character. For example: 'she made these allegations to get back at me', 'she said this to get me out of the house' (often regarding a stepdaughter).

Psychological Denial

No attempt is made to refute specific allegations but a more generalised response is given. For example: to suggest forcibly that ' I am not a person who would do such things'. This typically involves the collusions of friends and family who may well genuinely believed the protestations of innocence.

Minimisation of the extent of the behaviour

Virtually all abusers' admittance of their behaviour will be partial, particularly at initial assessment stage. Such minimisation may relate to the frequency and nature of the abusive acts and to the number of victims involved. Typically, the degree of risk posed in the future will be underestimated.

Denial of the seriousness of the behaviour

Due to the cognitive distortions utilised during offending, abusers normally have great difficulty in acknowledging the impact of their behaviour on their victims and its long term consequences. Often linked with this is the denial of the need for treatment.

Denial of responsibility

Abusers often admit their abusive behaviour and acknowledge its harmful effects but view themselves as the victim of circumstances. The denial typically involves arrays of mitigating circumstances – for example stress, alcohol, sexual frustration – and a refusal to accept that planning took place. 'It just happened', 'something came over me'.

Denial, as a component of the addictive assault cycle can be most difficult to tackle. Abusers will often continue to deny it despite the consequences, clear evidence to the contrary from victim statements, and having acknowledged the issue of contention in a previous session. They deny in order to defend their habituated or addictive behaviour both to themselves and to others. And also in some cases to prevent having to face the enormity of the damage they have inflicted upon children.

Working with denial

In assessment and subsequent intervention, effective working to reduce denial is clearly of the utmost importance. Care must be taken to avoid either collusion with the rationalising cognitions that are presented, or a directly confrontational approach which may back the abuser irretrievably into a corner. It is essential that workers allow an abuser to state his or her perceptions and understandings of the behaviour before the process of challenging begins. To avoid creating a situation which is abusive in itself, challenge should ideally take place within the context of the developed relationship between the abuser and the worker in which the former has a degree of confidence in the latter and in the process.

However, this may not be possible if the timescale of the intervention is limited to, for example, the preparation of a court report, or where child protection concerns require immediate decision-making. Direct confrontations should be used sparingly, and their timing may be critical.

In order to avoid being drawn into counterproductive confrontation in long-term interventions it is helpful to have undertaken motivational work at the outset. This should aim to encourage the abuser to understand the benefits and likely difficulties of engaging in the work and to produce an agreed contract. In considering motivational issues, the concept of ambivalence may be useful in understanding the potentially contradictory thoughts and feelings of the abuser: for example, 'I can change - there's no point in trying' 'I know I'm a risk - I can't afford to consider that I am a risk'. By persistently pushing a particularly challenging line that is met with resistance, workers run the risk of eliciting a response from the abuser which seeks to restore the equilibrium of their ambivalent feelings by arguing ever more strongly in disagreements. Miller and Rollnick (1991) provide invaluable instruction in the art of motivational interviewing.

Denial should also be understood in the context that we are asking the most personal and searching questions of perpetrators, if we posed questions about masturbation and illegal fantasy to any other type of client we would run the risk of a punch on the nose! It is hardly surprising then that in the initial stages of treatment we will find ourselves dealing with some degree of denial. We need to work gently with the perpetrator to reduce this, posing questions such as 'what is the worst thing you think you could say or that I could hear?'. Plenty of reassurance is required that there is nothing that they could say that you would not have heard before, and, that whilst you abhor their abusive behaviour, you are sure that there are lots of good parts to their makeup. Give lots of positive strokes when a move forward is made together with indirect challenges to information you do not believe. Do not say that you think they are lying but rather that you are confused or puzzled, as some things do not make sense and could they help you out?

In this work, many practitioners work from the assumptive stance that a perpetrator will have carried out more offences than we know about. Whilst this in general may be true, you may be working with a genuine first offender. It all had to start somewhere, even though our knowledge of sexual assaults cycles will suggest significant offence rehearsal in masturbation fantasy. With a first offender, the chances are likely to be good that you will be able to help the perpetrator change and develop enough relapse prevention strategies not to offend again. However, you will not do this if you constantly put forward the view that you think the client is lying. Miller's *Motivational Interviewing* (1991) is a useful book for helping workers move into an interviewing framework which enables the client to move on, and which lessens the possibility of asking 'closed' or aggressive questions. A condensed version (NOTA, 1997) is available for those who do not have the time to read the full textbook.

Workers should guard against seeing ambivalence as a deliberate strategy to avoid addressing the issues necessary for a perpetrator to be safe. Workers must think about what it means for the perpetrators to begin to disclose the full extent of their abuse of children. This can be a very slow and painful process that can be likened to peeling the layers of an onion. As a worker, it can also certainly make you feel like crying at times!

Triggers

In work with perpetrators we need to elicit certain things before we can move on and help them develop an armoury of relapse prevention techniques. We need to know what the trigger to offending is: is there a pattern? does the same thing trigger an instance of abuse or does the trigger change? Obviously, a perpetrator whose trigger is always the same has a better chance of identifying and controlling their behaviour than one who has many triggers. Triggers can be anything that affects the self esteem of the perpetrator. It can be an argument with a partner or a real or imagined slight from friends, relatives, acquaintances and work colleagues. Care must be taken because some perpetrators will engineer a trigger situation in order to give themselves permission to abuse. This may be motivated to get some form of revenge against the person who has been perceived to slight them or to prove to themselves that they have and are able to exert power over people, albeit children.. A row with a partner may give permission to abuse a child, thus taking revenge and wielding power and bolstering up a reduced self esteem.

Those who use alcohol or drugs as a disinhibitor should stop or rigidly control their drinking. For this they may need a referral to the nearest substance abuse centre.

Masturbation and fantasy

If an abuser wishes to make a serious effort to change and control his behaviour, workers need to find out what his masturbatory practices are and what sort of pornography is used. Illegal and legal fantasies will need to be discussed to obtain a picture of the relative proportion of each. Workers also need to know what aspects of previous child sexual abusive incidents are used within the fantasy and how long ago these took place. The work will have to take place within the usual child protection caveat on confidentiality, in that if you find out that a child is being hurt in the here and know you will have to pass this information to the relevant authorities.

Work in depth in this area can be very demanding and

threatening to all involved. Our advice is that it should take place in the context of an established professional relationship with the client, one in which motivational work has been undertaken and a clear contract drawn up, with the full involvement of the client.

Grooming

How a perpetrator grooms a victim is an essential part of their self knowledge for safety in relapse prevention. Do they spend years grooming or a short time? Who are their preferred victims? Are they intra-familial abusers or do they strike at strangers? What is the length of time between trigger, spotting a victim, grooming and the abuse? This is important in terms of relapse prevention because if it is a fairly long time the perpetrator has more time to acknowledge what is happening and get help in order not to offend again and create another victim.

There are many techniques used in grooming the environment and potential victims. As described earlier perpetrators may spend years grooming in, for example, the scouting and guiding movements, in church organisations, schools and residential institutions for children who have already suffered abuse and removal from their carers. All child abuse is a monstrous act against children but the organisational abuse of victims in the care system seems particularly abhorrent. Several years ago, Lynda was involved in working with the victims and colleagues of a senior youth worker who had had a long career of severely abusing the boys he was supposed to be youth working. When three young men finally came forward and disclosed, the worker had been abusing for almost 20 years and we will never know the full extent of the damage he caused. He was charged by the police, and upon being bailed, drove to the seaside and committed suicide. This was devastating for the young men who had disclosed, as it left an element of doubt for some people. This senior youth worker had groomed both the environment and the boys and staff so well that he was able to take a boy around the back of the building and bugger him after asking one of his junior workers to keep an eye on things. When a picture began to emerge of the extent of the abuse and the whens and wheres, many of the workers were overcome because they realised that it had been happening for years under their noses. Some workers had been suspicious because of the pool table and jukebox he had in the basement of his house to which the boys, never girls, had open access. One worker had been suspicious as she felt he was supplying cannabis to some boys. Another worker felt that abuse was going on after two partial disclosures over the years. She had spoken to the abusers senior manager who dismissed the thought out of hand, saying it was just the crazy way that the abuser worked and that everyone loved him and that perhaps she was jealous.

After the investigation which uncovered years of serious abuse we had to work with the workers for a considerable time as well as the victims. Some workers felt guilty because they had repressed suspicions and others felt guilty that they had not noticed. All felt tremendous anger at the damage that had been perpetrated on countless young men over a period of 20 years.

Perpetrators can be very very skilled at grooming people and the environment so that abuse can occur. When you begin to work with them, they will invariably use this often well honed skill on *you* in an attempt to manipulate the contents of the sessions and your view of them and their actions.

Common tactics include: encouraging workers to feel sorry for them as victims of circumstance who had no intention of hurting anyone; asserting that now they have been apprehended they have learnt their lesson and will pose no risk in the future; or suggesting that workers are finding the discussion of such intimate matters embarrassing or upsetting.

Sometimes perpetrators adopt an overtly aggressive stance towards workers, questioning their skills and authority to undertake the work. If the workers are co-working the perpetrator may try to make an alliance with one worker, thereby de-skilling the other; this can be a feature in mixed gender co-working relationships and should be thoroughly discussed before the work is undertaken. On occasion, anger may be employed in an attempt to disempower workers and generate 'stand-offs' which are in turn used as evidence of the workers' lack of competence.

- Patience and an ability to avoid being drawn into such interactions are essential skills in undertaking the work.

- Be aware, always work in pairs and make use of supervision or peer group support.
- Ensure that the work is well planned and that the co-working relationship is healthy, open and supportive.

The abuse

The obvious point at which to start work with an abuser (once they have been motivated and contracting has been undertaken) is an exploration of the known incidents of abuse. It is important when building up a picture to facilitate relapse prevention work that you are fully aware of the type of abuse perpetrated by the person you are working with. Typically this awareness is achieved by encouraging the abuser to 'tell the story of their abusive behaviour' and to amend and expand on this with the help of victim statements made to the police, what the victim may be saying in therapy and further reflection by the abuser.

Getting an understanding of the true nature of the abuse can be difficult and workers need to employ all the strategies that they can. It is important to read the victim account if at all possible, and, if it is an old case, to contact the arresting officers as they may remember what the victim said. If it is a new case then contact the Crown Prosecution Service to get release of the documents or again speak to the arresting police officers from the Child Protection Unit. In all cases, working in partnership with the child's social worker will be invaluable and will also keep you in touch with the notion that work with perpetrators is a crucial facet of child protection and therefore of safeguarding children.

The belief is false that non-contact abuse such as flashing or voyeurism is less serious than 'hands on abuse'. Different victims react differently to abuse, and it is the reaction that is important. Moreover if you look at the history of some very dangerous men, such as Robert Black, you will find that they began with non-contact offences, adding the experience to their fantasies for masturbation. As the 'softer' abuse failed to excite them, they began to add more serious abuse to their fantasy and then eventually to act them out. In this way sexual abuse is analogous to addiction – the addict craves a bigger and bigger fix as time goes on.

Victim empathy

Our knowledge of the use of cognitive distortions in abusing would suggest that if the perpetrator can understand what it feels like to be a victim then this should enable internal and external inhibitors to be activated. Victim empathy can, therefore, be a powerful tool in enabling the development of internal inhibitors to abuse, and thus preventing the perpetrator offending again. It is important that this work is undertaken during every stage of the work with a perpetrator.

The perpetrator needs to understand in absolute detail the cognitive distortions that enabled them to commit the abuse in the beginning. They need to feel shame. Shame is a stronger emotion than guilt, which is often predicated on externals such as being caught or what people may think. Shame evidences internalisation of the consequences of the abuse on the victim and the part that the perpetrator plays in this. (That it is *solely* the responsibility of the perpetrator and *not in any way* the responsibility of the victim). It is only when full responsibility is accepted and shame is felt that perpetrators are able to begin to feel victim empathy and really to begin to understand the harm they have caused. This is a difficult stage to reach and many will get no further than a transitory guilt following the abuse, feelings of self-pity, and even anger at the victim because they have been caught and have to face the consequences.

Undertaking victim empathy work is notoriously difficult and its timing is crucial if the encouragement of 'poor me' feelings and continued anger is to be avoided. It is often useful to gain a 'snapshot' of an abuser's understanding of victim's feelings at an early stage in the work in order to provide a marker for future progress (or lack of it!). However, views thus given should not be directly or aggressively challenged at this point, but merely noted. This often requires considerable self control on the part of the workers who may well feel incensed at the apparent callousness or naivety expressed by the perpetrator. Confrontation at such a point is more likely to entrench such views than to encourage an abuser to examine them critically.

Moreover, to be fruitful, victim empathy work should not be undertaken in any depth until an abuser has made significant progress in acknowledging the nature and extent of the abusive behaviour and in dismantling defence mechanisms employed as cognitive distortions. Bear in mind that in order to inflict such damage on children abusers must have very well developed cognitive distortions that prevent them putting themselves in the place of their victims and therefore feeling any sort of empathy.

A further note of caution is necessary. *If there is evidence or suspicion that an abuser's motivation to offend includes sadistic components, victim empathy work should be avoided.* If such abusers are encouraged to gain a better appreciation of the distress and harm caused to victims this may have an unintended effect of further reinforcing their abusive fantasies and feelings of sexual gratification. This may result in increasing their propensity to sexually abuse rather than diminish it!

There are many strategies for bringing about victim empathy, for example writing a letter to the victims (usually not to be sent!), meeting with victims (not their own) and looking at videos of victims speaking about their experience. This direct work with victims should not begin until the worker has absolute evidence that the perpetrator is beginning to change how they think, feel and behave. However if victim empathy is achieved then there is solid ground upon which to begin to develop relapse prevention strategies. These will be different for each perpetrator and need to be realistic and easily used.

Changes to be encouraged in abusers

The development of victim empathy requires the perpetrator's thinking, feeling and doing to be in congruence. It is not enough for them to say that they understand their impact on their victim within a session; there must be observable and reportable changes in the behaviour and attitudes of the perpetrator. They have to demonstrate that they have permanently changed their life style, often to the extent of finding new friends and forming relationships with people who are not involved in the abuse of children. They will have to stop using child pornography. It may be impossible to stop the use of pornography entirely so the perpetrator needs to use that which depicts consenting adults. We do not propose to enter into the debate about pornography here, only to say that in this work adult pornography can, in some controlled circumstances, be useful in weaning men and women off child pornography. However, this work should *only* be undertaken by suitably qualified and experienced practitioners.

For some, changes of address and perhaps changes in employment may be required if either bring them into regular unsupervised contact with children.

A fair proportion of schedule 1 sex offenders 'get religion' while in prison. Without detracting from those who have genuine religious beliefs, we would raise a note of caution. The message of forgiveness and redemption given by the church, may be inappropriately comforting for perpetrators. Many feel that this is enough and they then do not need to enter into the type of work described in this book. This is a fallacy, and is just another way for perpetrators to avoid treatment and the need to face the uncomfortable reality of their actions. If the faith is real, it will help to motivate an individual in the treatment and not serve as an excuse to avoid undertaking difficult, uncomfortable and personally threatening work.

Relapse prevention

Relapse prevention runs right through work with perpetrators and should begin as soon as the initial assessment is complete. In its initial stages it can draw on the perpetrator's wish not to suffer the consequences of further allegations and arrest, and is likely to concentrate on blanket avoidance strategies and external controls. Examples may include: no unsupervised contact with any children; continuing to live outside the family home; frequent reminders of the consequences of further abuse in an attempt to restrict reinforcing sexual arousal and inappropriate sexual fantasies etc.

In the longer term more sophisticated and, hopefully more effective, relapse prevention packages can be developed, informed by the work undertaken on the nature of an individual's abusive behaviour.

To be successful, the work should build on both external and internal controls, the perpetrator attempting to modify his internal and external behaviour. Monitoring of sexual arousal patterns through the use of 'masturbation diaries' that indicate the frequency of masturbation and the types of fantasies being used can alert an abuser when there might be an increasing risk of the cycle being triggered. At the point when the cycle would be triggered, then the perpetrator needs to respond to this by informing others (external controls) and substituting another activity, rather than going further into fantasy and masturbatory rehearsal. A choice could be made to participate in displacement activity. This could be anything from listening to music, going shopping or seeking out social situations with friends who are not linked to the past abusive behaviours. The phone number for an emergency line may be given, so that if the perpetrator is experiencing difficulty in coming out of the cycle immediate counselling support is available.

Regular attendance at a relapse prevention group or regular contact with the worker who understands the perpetrator is necessary at this stage until the perpetrator, and indeed the protection services, have confidence in the ability of the perpetrator to use relapse prevention techniques effectively to significantly reduce the risk of creating more victims. Both worker and perpetrator need to understand that in the beginning there will be *lapses* when the cycle will be entered. However, so long as *relapse* (that is a further incident of abuse) is prevented this can be used as a learning experience in that it will give clues to the areas of relapse prevention that need strengthening for that particular perpetrator.

The work must as always take place in a framework of inter-agency cooperation and information sharing and none should lose sight of the purpose of the work – to protect children from sexual abuse. At this stage the worker must take a central role in the management of risk and also act immediately if there is evidence that relapse has or is happening.

Risk is looked at in depth in the following chapters. Managing risk can be difficult. Workers sometimes feel that they have the responsibility for preventing perpetrators from sexually abusing children. They should remember that the perpetrator is responsible for their actions and if they choose to abuse then the responsibility is the perpetrator's alone. The worker is responsible for undertaking a realistic risk assessment that will decide whether the risk can be managed in the circumstances proposed and to monitor any arrangements subsequently made to the best of their professional ability.

Rehabilitation

Workers may have to do an assessment for family rehabilitation in two different types of circumstance. The first is when a schedule 1 sex offender wishes to return to the family where the abuse was perpetrated. The other is when an offender wishes to move into a new family where there are children. The chapters on risk assessment look in more detail at the issues involved in making professional judgements in these situations. Here we need to look at the issues underpinning the possibility of rehabilitation and the process whereby this would happen. Looking at rehabilitation of an abusive adult to the family where abuse took place, we need to consider several factors of equal importance. The effect on the victim, both at the time of the abuse and at the time of the proposed rehabilitation, needs to be looked at carefully to ensure that the children are expressing their own views and not the views of the parents.

Children who have been abused can feel a very wide range of emotions. For some there is guilt at the perpetrator serving a prison sentence. The victim may not have wanted this – they may just have wanted the abuse to stop. There may be conflicting emotions towards the parents and the child protection workers. The child or children should have designated workers independent from those of the parents during the time that rehabilitation is being considered. They need to be able to speak in their true voice and not state things that they think others want to hear.

In one recent case the child felt guilty that her stepfather had gone to prison. This had also upset her mother, even though her mother and had acted in the child's best interests and reported the abuse to the police in the first place. The child was very confused because she witnessed her disabled mother's struggle while her partner was in prison. Upon release, the mother was saying quite clearly that she wanted the incident forgotten and the resumption of 'normal' family life. She felt that the child protection services were making things worse by working with the child and not allowing contact with the stepfather. As far as she was concerned, the partner was attending the groupwork sessions and sessions with his probation officer, and keeping them apart was causing more damage. It took 12 sessions with the child before she was able to articulate that she did not want her stepfather home. She was frightened of him, and felt she needed a lot of evidence that a part of him had truly gone before she could alter these views. At this point her mother became very angry with the therapeutic workers saying that we had made her child say this, that they had the Church and that they did not need outside interference. This would appear to be a case of the mother, despite acting in the child's best interests at first disclosure, allowing her need for her partner to take precedence over her daughter's needs. As such, concerns were raised about her future ability to protect the child and her apparent minimising of serious oral and penetrative abuse.

The multi-agency group of workers were agreed that they were unable to recommend rehabilitation in these circumstances, as, despite ongoing work with the mother, she was unable to put her child first and then act on a realistic view of the risks that might be imposed by rehabilitation.

In another case the child initially disclosed at school, and upon being informed, the mother acted appropriately, for she was quite clear with her husband that the five children came first and only had letter contact with him during his prison sentence. When he was released he volunteered for the community treatment programme and she was involved in this. Each step was agreed and when they both felt that there were fully aware of the cycle and also the signs that would indicate he was lapsing and possibly heading for relapse, a series of supervised and controlled contacts were set up outside the family home. Each step was discussed and evaluated by all concerned, and the mother encouraged the children to express any concerns or feelings that they had towards their father. This process took two years, after which the family were re-united. To this day the father attends relapse prevention sessions, despite at times during the process feeling angry and frustrated. However, the parents worked in full cooperation with the child protection services and probation. The family are still together and the father has not, to anyone's knowledge, abused. They do sometimes liken their life to living in a goldfish bowl, but recognise that this is a small price to pay for keeping their children safe and the father out of prison.

The difference in these two cases was that the father in the second case was able to accept responsibility for what he had done and did not attempt to minimise or deny. This is not to say that his level of understanding had always been this good. For him, it was like peeling off the layers of an onion. He had a level of denial and cognitive distortion in the beginning. It took him a long time to fully acknowledge his grooming of the internal environment, including his wife, and the lengths to which he had gone to be alone with his youngest child. As he painstakingly developed the level of understanding, this was shared with his wife who built up a realistic picture of his offending behaviour. At the same time they undertook sessions on parenting skills together and also did some couple work so they were able to begin to communicate effectively and sort out their problems. The professionals involved ensured that information was shared and the worker with the children had a full account of all new information and understanding. In fact the mother became the conduit for this information, being given the task through the core group in recognition of the importance of her role and contribution to the process.

The key factor in the success story was the recognition by both parents that there was a lot of work to do and they needed to understand the hows and whys of the abuse together in order to keep the children safe. This meant a full recognition of all the painful facets of this, rather than minimisation and denial.

Child sexual abuse will not go away; if ignored it is the canker that grows in ignorance. For some it may seem that the level of work needed in the second case cannot be sustained. However, spread between agencies it is manageable, and means the family are reunited and the abuser is not a 'loose cannon' moving in on a new family and abusing again. Moreover, the child will have felt reassured that the allegations did not result in the break-up of her family with all its attendant distress. Multi-agency fora need to look at preventative and therapeutic work so that we may begin to reduce the number of victims. In the long run, this would reduce the economic cost of child sex abuse, but more importantly prevent more children undergoing abuse.

In the first case there was denial on the part of both parents.

The abuser colluded with the mother's wish to minimise and forget. He remained at a level of denial and minimisation that blamed everything else in his life, even his former wife for the abuse. The mother felt that going to Church together would ensure that abuse did not happen again. In all this neither seriously considered how the victim or her brother were feeling. In this case the parents' collusion meant that rehabilitation could never be considered. They would have to remain apart until the children reached their majority.

For the worker, these decisions can be very difficult. However, they should not be the responsibility of just one worker, but of the core group constituted under the child protection process. Considering the rehabilitation of an abuser back into his or her family, while generating high levels of anxiety in professionals, may, in some situations, be in the long term best interests of children. We hope that the knowledge base presented in this book will increase practitioners' confidence in determining when such rehabilitation might be possible and in identifying the safeguards that would be required.

With families where a schedule 1 offender wants to, or has moved in, the issues are different. Firstly, the known victim is not in the family, though this does not mean that a victim from another perpetrator is not in the family. The decision around rehabilitation would depend on the honesty of the perpetrator and what sort of therapeutic work, if any, they have done on their abusing. Is it a genuine case of a relationship developing or is it part of the perpetrator's grooming technique, the parent being used in order to get access to the children? A view can be reached about this quite quickly in terms of the information given to the non-abusive partner about previous abuse and the reaction to the involvement of child protection services.

The attitude of the non-abusing partner to the abuse and the abuser are important. Do they understand the full import of the information that they have been given, and can they evaluate in realistic terms the risk to their family, and the measures that are needed to ensure the children are not abused? In all cases the worker will need to work with all agencies involved and painstakingly gather information from all the available sources. The risk assessments and decisions about appropriate action and recommendations for work with both adults should be taken collectively by the core group and not a singleton worker. Thus, the child protection system should work in partnership to ensure that decision making is rational and the level of risk involved is both containable and manageable.

Supervision and support

When working in any areas of child protection, and most particularly in work with schedule 1 sex offenders, it is extremely important that the worker receives a good level of supervision and support. Sadly, for some this is not available from their direct line managers for a variety of reasons. I would strongly suggest in this case that workers negotiate with management to ensure that they get the appropriate level of supervision necessary for this work. It is necessary that those people supervising and managing workers in this field understand the difficult nature of the work and the possible impact it can have on workers. It may be appropriate to offer workers same sex supervision so that they are freely able to discuss impact issues around their own sexuality and their sexual relationships with their partners. We would argue that workers going into this field should be given a health warning stating that working with perpetrators of child sexual abuse can have a serious detrimental effect on the workers own sex life! Female workers may need to access to a female line manager or consultant if their supervision is by a male manager. This may be necessary given that a female worker may spend her working life in a room with a group of schedule 1 sex offenders who are often male, and her co-worker may also be male.

Male workers will also need skilled and sensitive supervision. It can be difficult for male workers to sit and listen to fantasies articulated by the group members if they bear some similarity to those that they experience themselves. It can be extremely uncomfortable for male workers to experience this and may lead them to question their own behaviour within sexual relationships. Of course this also applies to female workers working with female abusers.

Because there are areas of this work that people in general find difficult to talk about we would strongly recommend that supervisors attend courses directly related to supervising workers who are working with schedule 1 sex offenders.

In the same way we would also recommend that mixed gender co-workers who work together consult with a consultant or supervisor in order to ensure that the co-working relationship is healthy and honest from the outset, and that they will be able to deal with any difficulties in a rational and professional manner. This should include them being able to state clearly that either of them feels that there is a barrier to them working effectively together. At the beginning of the co-working relationship it is often helpful to have the supervisor, a consultant or another person involved in the initial co-working exercises, and in the development of the agreements for the preliminary and the de-briefing procedures to be undertaken as part of the planning of the work. All stages of planning are important. However, for the psychological health of the worker we feel that de-briefing is crucial, so that the workers do not take the work home to 'taint' their family environment.

Finally, we would also argue that a strong sense of humour and supportive colleagues are a requisite to undertaking this work if burn-out is to be avoided.

Summary

The main issues to be taken into account when working with perpetrators may be summarised as follows:

- Working with perpetrators is an integral component of child protection. The responsibility for the work belongs to the core group who should ensure, via the designated key worker for the case, that clear and effective communication takes place between all interested parties. The work should be multi-disciplinary and multi-agency with all workers working to the same standards and criteria.
- Workers need skilled supervision.
- Co-working should be the norm unless there are sound professional reasons not to.

- Workers need to be aware at all times that abusers are generally very skilled at grooming and manipulation and will attempt to use these skills on the workers in order to undermine their effectiveness.
- Workers need a good understanding of the sexual assault cycle and how to work with distorted thinking.
- Workers need to understand how perpetrators can change and how to assess and manage risk.
- Managers and supervisors need to be skilled in the supervision and support of workers in this difficult field.
- Managers, supervisors and workers need competent training in working with the sexual abusers of children. This should be updated regularly.

Chapter 4

Assessment of risk in family situations

AS OUR understanding of sexually abusive behaviour has developed (and with it an increasingly sophisticated knowledge that such behaviour may continue and indeed escalate), so case conferences and the civil and criminal courts have sought assessments of risk in attempts to reduce the likelihood of further sexual abuse of children. As with any predictions of human behaviour, many factors could/should be taken into account and making definitive projections is almost impossible. Unfortunately, practitioners will be only too aware of the ease with which assessments of 'high risk' can be made in retrospect i.e. once behaviour has escalated to the point where official sanction is again triggered - and after a considerable amount of victimisation has been suffered.

This chapter considers the issues that should be taken into account when undertaking or reviewing assessments of risk and suggests methods that are likely to increase the rigorousness of the process and hopefully the accuracy and usefulness of conclusions reached.

Although this book explicitly sets out to 'demystify' work with sexual abusers, it would be quite wrong to encourage practitioners with little or no experience in this area of work to undertake risk assessments. We would emphasise the need for a good understanding of the knowledge base and the development of specific skills in assessment (practised and refined on a regular basis). Non-specialists should seek appropriate training, undertake appropriate reading and offer to co-work with practitioners who have developed a degree of specialism. Further comments on ensuring that the practice of assessment is undertaken in a safe and professionally acceptable manner are made in chapter 7.

Risk and sexual abusers

How does our generalised theoretical, research and clinical knowledge base help us to determine risk in individual cases, in particular circumstances?

Over the past 20 years we have come to realise that sexual abuse is a serious social problem and that a significant proportion of abusers will have multiple victims, experience repetitive urges to abuse and constitute a very high risk indeed. Where 'high risk' is established it is usually clear that intervention must concentrate on control (rather than change), and that practitioners should get on with the task of engaging the abuser in monitoring and avoidance strategies. But many other abusers pose a risk that is more difficult to quantify, and many of these will have the potential to continue to victimise and abuse. The obvious point that abusers of multiple victims will have started with 'only' one victim is not lost on practitioners and, for obvious reasons causes much anxiety. Although we have developed a much better understanding of the factors that should be taken into account in determining risk, making a judgement in individual situations is still a complex and problematic task.

It is to be hoped that current research into 'typologies' of sexual abusers will be able to aid the prediction of risk and already we do have some pointers. Despite acknowledging that reconviction rates are likely to grossly underestimate the situation, they indicate variable recidivism for abusers in different situations:

Incest perpetrators 4-10 % (Gibbons, Soothil & Way, 1978; 1981)
Extrafamilial perpetrators against girls 10-20 % (Furby et al, 1989)
Extrafamilial perpetrators against boys 13-40 % (Furby et al, 1989)

These figures could suggest that those abusing within a family are relatively less likely to re-abuse and that it will often be possible to manage family rehabilitation successfully and positively for all concerned. Although this may be so in some cases, it should not escape assessors that family situations are those which offer considerable potential for an abuser to wield power and manipulate both adults and children. It may be that in such situations victims feel unable to speak out again, or decide that enduring further abuse is preferable to the trauma of further allegations and investigations. Concern that official figures may be distorted by these phenomena are given credence by studies which strongly suggest that most sexual abuse occurs within family situations rather than outside of them (see chapter 1).

The relative increased riskiness of abusers of boys outside of family situations is borne out by other studies (Sinclair, 1991), and may relate to men commonly described as 'paedophiles'. Such men often have a belief system that sexual attraction to children is positive and to be promoted. They are often highly fixated in this and associated behaviours, and may construct their day to day lives around this interest. Given the likely pervasiveness of such behaviour it would be surprising if this group did not represent a high level of risk. Moreover, this type of abuser often works within groups or 'rings', sharing child pornography and victims.

The 'seriousness' of known abuse is often a significant factor in deciding risk. Abuse which involves physical assaults and obvious trauma to victims will be viewed with particular concern. Assumptions will typically be made that this equates with potential 'dangerousness' and may indicate a significant loss of control on the part of the abuser. However, our knowledge of the range of sexually abusive behaviours informs us that many equally serious forms of abuse are more subtle, generating guilt, low self esteem and self destructive behaviours in victims. Assessing the impact of grooming on victims is an important task in developing insight into the nature of the harm done, particularly when considering family rehabilitation. The harm done does not necessarily correlate to the 'seriousness' of the abuse. Victim impact is determined by many factors of which this is just one.

The length of time over which known abuse has been previously perpetrated will contribute to an assessment of seriousness. Extensive grooming and an increasing preoccupation with abusing will frequently be revealed in assessments of such situations, suggesting entrenched patterns of thoughts, feelings, fantasies and behaviour which may prove particularly resistant to change.

Practitioners are more likely to view situations where abuse has been identified as occurring on 'only' a few occasions as potentially manageable in the future, but will worry about whether they have simply been denied a more accurate picture of its extent.

Assessments are usually expected to comment on how risk may change over time, which can prove a particularly difficult issue in the context of our child protection system, where interventions are increasingly expected to be time limited. For example, many assessments suggest that whilst the current risk may be 'low' and/ or 'manageable' due to the children in the family being significantly younger than previous known victims, the risk in the longer term, as these children grow older, may increase significantly.

There is some evidence to suggest that risk of reoffending for convicted child sex offenders can increase significantly over time. Marshall & Barbaree (1990) found that of a group of 'treated' offenders 5.5% had re offended after 2 years, 25% after 4 years. The corresponding figures for the control group of 'untreated' offenders make even more depressing reading - 12.5% re offended after 2 years, 64% after 4 years. This study also raises the all important question of the efficacy of 'treatment' programmes. Participation in such schemes should not, in itself, be viewed as reducing risk, but feedback from them is often useful in analysing risk and in monitoring attempts at its management. Abusers who commence and subsequently drop out of treatment are viewed as constituting an increased risk (Abel, 1988), although this may merely be a reflection of their resistance to change and 'riskiness' per se.

'Cross over' (Abel & Rouleau, 1990) refers to the abuse of victims of different types, particularly by gender and age. Evidence of 'cross over' is likely to generate increasing concerns that the subject may at times experience relatively indiscriminate arousal and pose a high degree of risk to a wide group of victims. It must be stressed, however, that the corollary to this is not valid - a lack of evidence of 'crossover' cannot be equated with 'no risk' to children of the opposite gender to those previously abused. There is little doubt, though, that many practitioners would feel more optimistic about the potential for safe management of risk in a family where children were of different ages and/or gender to previous victims.

The more varied the nature of previous known abuse in terms of types of: victims (age, gender); situations (family, institution, public places); relationships (parent/child, abuser/stranger) the more likely that an assessment of high risk will be made. But for many assessments such certainty is impossible, due to a lack of crucial information, to the absence of conclusive indicators or the presence of conflicting factors. Assessments often have to be 'the best possible under the circumstances' and seek to achieve an acceptable balance between the needs of children and the rights of adults.

Our understanding of sexually abusive behaviour and the risk of further abuse posed by individuals is clearly still in its infancy. Moreover, the knowledge we do have is to some extent contradictory. Official statistics (including conviction rates) appear to 'play down' levels of abuse and risk of recidivism, whilst our theoretical models tend to emphasise the potential for further, and sometimes escalating, victimisation. In chapter 1 we have reviewed research findings that suggest that levels of sexual abuse in our society are significant (if not endemic) and that risk of continuing abuse following initial apprehension of an individual abuser must be taken seriously. Assessments of risk must acknowledge these uncertainties, and the decision making and planning based on them must be undertaken with caution and due care.

Assessing risk: What is the nature of the task?

As in work with sexual abusers in general, assessments are most useful when they comprise a detailed analysis of specific situations. Generalisations, however tempting it is to make them (especially in the face of limited information), should be used sparingly and treated with caution when applied to inform decision making. It may be useful to conceptualise assessment in the form of two key questions:

1. *What is the nature and extent of the risk posed in this situation?* 'To answer this question requires an analysis of known previous abusive behaviour and its implications for either the current (or proposed) family situation.

2. *What is the potential for its safe management?*
   This question requires assessment of the likely risks involved
   in the family situation, the damage that is likely to be caused
   to a child and the likely ability of individuals therein to
   acknowledge risk and co operate with its monitoring.

For many local authority social workers a third key question will
be posed - What are the costs / benefits of any intervention based on
the above analysis? Enquiries into abuse in residential children's
homes have highlighted the potential risks of removing children
from their families and placing them 'in care'. Once again workers
assessing what appears to be patterns of 'serious' abuse are more
likely to take the view that removal is the only realistic option
available, but will struggle with this dilemma in apparently 'less
serious' cases. It remains an indictment of our child care legislation
that it is difficult to remove from a family an adult whose risk is
assessed as significant, especially in situations where a criminal
conviction is not sought or obtained. Workers are often left with no
option than to threaten care proceedings and, if this pressure is
unsuccessful, apply to the courts for removal of the children.

In the face of these tensions and dilemmas, it is even more
important that evaluations of risk are essentially child rather than
adult focused (despite the fact that much of the information
gathered will relate to the adults in a family), and that the scope
and purpose of assessments are clearly defined. Briggs et al (1997,
pp.144-5) suggest that the following parameters need to be
ascertained:

1. Who are the subjects and objects of risk assessment, i.e. who,
   and in what combination are considered as potential abusers,
   and of whom?
2. The form of risk to be assessed should be identified, including
   not only issues of direct sexual abuse and indirect sexual
   abuse......, but also the broader spectrum of abuses, including
   emotional abuse, neglect and physical abuse.
3. Some idea of the circumstances under which the abuse may or
   may not be expected to occur should be determined, i.e. the
   questions of 'when?' and 'where?'
4. In addition, and if possible, attempts should be made to
   describe the likely mechanics of abuse, (the 'how?' question)

including the potential targeting and grooming procedures which might be used.

What can be expected of risk assessments ?

The preceding sections indicate the complexity and potential pitfalls of making pronouncements on risk, and caution is advocated in undertaking assessments and interpreting their conclusions. Despite much progress, the assessment of risk is far from constituting an exact science and remains in itself 'a risky business' (Morrison & Print, 1995). At best, assessments should be viewed as informed professional opinions, the quality of which will be dependent on: the skills, knowledge and experience of the assessors; the rigour with which the assessment process is undertaken; and luck (particularly regarding the availability of relevant information). Research undertaken on the efficacy of clinical judgement is not particularly encouraging (Thornton, 1997) – a fact which underlines the need for assessments to be accessible to others and for subsequent decision making to be made on a multi-agency basis.

Furthermore, 'risk' is not a static concept, so assessment will always be part of a continuing process of intervention. Risk is likely to change over time and in different circumstances. Assessments should address such variables to the best of your ability and should caution against interpretations of conclusions being viewed as automatically relevant over time. In fact, assessments can only become reasonably accurate by observing changes over time (particularly with regard to subjects' motivation to change) so as to monitor and control risk.

Before considering how risk might be assessed, it maybe useful to summarise the basic requirements for adequate evaluations (which should inform those who are undertaking assessments and aid the interpretation of assessments provided by others). Assessments should:

1. be grounded in known base rates of sexual abuse (while acknowledging the far from complete picture currently available)

2. be informed by current theoretical understanding and clinical experience
3. involve a structured process of information gathering (which is time consuming and resource intensive)
4. gather information in an ordered, structured and accessible manner (to allow others to comment from an informed position)
5. be detailed and seek to:
    a. identify the nature and extent of risk posed (to whom, in what circumstances, and with what likely effect?)
    b. analyse the potential (and mechanics) for risk management (how, by whom?)
6. generate conclusions from the key factors identified from the process of assessment (the approach should be transparent - to allow others to challenge)
7. explore alternative explanations and conclusions
8. clearly state likely limitations and possible weaknesses of the process employed (particularly regarding lack of information and the need for specialist input)
9. identify clearly further work required (and, if possible, by whom it will be undertaken)
10. detail the response of those assessed to the conclusions drawn.

Ways of assessing risk

Past behaviour is undoubtedly the best available indicator of future risk and its analysis should form the core of any assessment. Quinsey, Rice and Harris (1995) suggest that risk assessments should be based on static variables (eg. known previous abuse, personal history), and then modified by consideration of dynamic variables (eg. potential for treatment/change, monitoring arrangements). Such an approach seems entirely appropriate. It would hardly be justifiable, for example, to assess risk as 'manageable' in a situation where a family appear particularly cooperative but where there remained a lack of basic understanding about the nature of the risk posed. How effective can monitoring be when the thing we are trying to avoid is poorly understood? How would we know whether we were monitoring the right things or interpreting behaviour correctly?

A well used framework is that of Brearley (1982), who suggests that risk can be evaluated through use of the following model:

1. Predisposing hazards (which equate with static variables)
2. Situational hazards (external pressures/disruptions)
3. Strengths which may counteract the risks
4. Dangers (who is at risk and in what way?)

Access to relevant information is a crucial factor in determining whether accurate assessments can be made, and assessors should use a wide range of sources. The greater the number of sources, the better the potential for cross checking facts, and providing some corroboration for significant variables identified. Sources typically include:

- Criminal records and child care proceedings in the civil court
- Statements made to the police (abuser, partner, victims - including video evidence)
- Agency records (Social Services, Probation, Health, Housing, Hostels, Prisons)
- Self report from those who are the subject of assessment (abuser, partner, children)
- Questionnaires
- Monitoring and observation by others
- Previous response to assessment / treatment (if relevant)
- Psychological assessment
- Penile Plethysmograph

Some of these sources are more readily available than others, but unless a subject has been previously apprehended for sexual abuse it is likely that information will be limited so that assessors will have to rely heavily on self report in order to form a reasonably rounded view of the issues involved. The difficulties this represents, given our understanding of the role of cognitive distortions in sexually abusive behaviour, will be discussed in greater detail in chapter 7.

Even when information is more freely available, making sense of it can be a daunting task. Assessors will sometimes feel overwhelmed by the array of incidents to examine, factors to consider and patterns to discern. Recognising the need for rigour in situations where decisions have a significant impact on individuals, most practitioners favour the use of some form of risk assessment 'tool' that orders information in a professionally recognised manner and contributes to a quantification of risk.

Models for assessing risk

Many 'models' and 'formats' have been developed by various agencies and disciplines to address risk assessment in different settings. Some attempts to provide exact measures of 'riskiness' are available. These often comprise a checklist of factors that are given a numerical factor of seriousness, with conclusions generated by the addition of all the points 'scored'. This typically results in abusers being placed in apparently discrete categories such as 'low', 'medium' and 'high'. Given the importance of assessing information in the light of the whole knowledge base regarding sexually abusive behaviour and the need to evaluate dynamics between variables, such mechanistic approaches should be treated with the utmost caution. Their use can have serious consequences if a false sense of security is generated by a low score and an unsafe assessment of 'low risk'. Furthermore, the simplistic nature of these instruments can encourage practitioners with little relevant experience to make pronouncements on risk - a practice that is risky indeed!

More rigorous methods of categorisation into 'low', 'medium' and 'high' risk exist which encourage practitioners to evaluate the information gathered, form professional judgements about their salience and monitor movement between categories over time (eg Beckett, 1995; Fisher & Thornton, 1993). These have developed an algorithm which can be useful to gain an appreciation of static variables based on a subject's criminal record:

A point is awarded for each of the following indicators:

- Any previous convictions for a sexual offence
- More than 4 previous convictions of any nature
- Any current of previous convictions for violence (non sexual)
- Preconvictions for sexual offences against 3 or more victims

Accumulation of points suggests the following categorisation:

0 = low risk
1 = low - medium
2 = medium - high
3 = high
4 = high +

Clearly practitioners would be particularly concerned about subjects who score 2 or more points, and this algorithm can help confirm that some people are undeniably high risk. As ever, attributions of low risk are more difficult to make with any confidence, given the algorithm's sole reliance on the criminal justice system as a source of data.

Other models avoid computational approaches, favouring frameworks which guide assessors to the types of information that they should be seeking and from which professional judgements should be made. Loss & Ross (1991), in an overview of their highly detailed assessment protocol for young abusers, identify 23 key factors to be examined:

1. Cooperation with the assessment process
2. Honesty and self initiated disclosure
3. Degree of aggression/sadism in abusive behaviour, responsiveness to victim's pain/ resistance
4. Frequency, duration and intensity of abuse
5. Length, nature and progression of sexual aggression
6. Offence characteristics other than aggression
7. Number of victims in relation to potential contact with victims
8. Victim selection characteristics
9. Intensity of arousal before, during and after assault
10. Nature and focus of masturbatory fantasies
11. Personal responsibility for abusive behaviour, understanding of wrongfulness
12. Precipitating and trigger factors - impulsiveness
13. Other abusive or addictive behaviours
14. Family system functioning
15. School / employment stability
16. Social relationships
17. Non offending sexual history and victimisation

18. External motivation / leverage for treatment and change
19. Internal motivation, ability to see patterns
20. Response to confrontation, willingness to abide by rules
21. Treatment history
22. Criminal arrests, convictions and institutional history
23. Current access to past, current or potential victims

One is impressed by the wide range of factors thought worthy of exploration, the depth of knowledge required to interpret their significance and the considerable array of skills necessary if assessment is to be competently undertaken. This type of approach builds on one of the key insights of the knowledge base that understanding sexually abusive behaviour should be multi-factoral. Chapter 5 will consider in some detail the use of multi-factor approaches in assessment. They have the double advantage of being straightforward to use without having any pretensions about being able to 'compute' degrees of risk on behalf of workers.

Chapter 5

Multifactor approaches to the assessment of risk and risk management

MULTI FACTOR FORMATS are designed to order the complex information that must be gathered before risk can be analysed. The frameworks can make the basic assumptions of any assessment more easily accessible to all those involved in the decision making processes and may be appended to reports for use in a variety of settings.

Despite their relative sophistication, we have misgivings about these formats, as agencies may require them to be used mechanistically and/or used by workers with insufficient training in the area of sexual abuse and with inadequate support. Safe use of formats assumes a level of familiarity with key theories of how abusers typically operate.

The 'Four step' model developed by David Finkelhor (1984) is used by many practitioners as the basis of a framework for ordering information gathered in the assessment process. This approach can be particularly useful when assessment is of an abuser within a particular defined social context (for example a family, where there maybe easily identifiable potential victims) and where a lack of information about previous incidents of abuse may render attempts to 'calculate' a level of risk less effective.

The variant of the underlying model described and demonstrated here takes as its reference point a multifactor assessment format developed over time by a number of practitioners and trainers (Donaghy & Gocke, 1995; Gocke &

Markham, 1997): The format comprises four main sections and is deliberately simple:

1.0 Basic information
1.1 Abuser's known abusive behaviour
1.2 Abuser's offending history
1.3 Abuser's personal circumstances / Background

2.0 Analysis of abusive behaviour
2.1 Abuser's sexual motivation to abuse
2.2 Abuser's overcoming of internal inhibitions
2.3 Abuser's circumvention of external inhibitors
2.4 Abuser's overcoming of victim resistance.

3.0 Analysis of current circumstances
3.1 Abuser's current sexual motivations
3.2 Abuser's maintenance of internal controls
3.3 Effectiveness of external controls
3.4 Potential victims.

4.0 Conclusions & assessment of risk

Section (1) and to some extent (2) equate in essence to the concept of 'static variables', whilst sections (3) refers to 'dynamic variables'. It is usually helpful to maintain these distinctions when applying the format, although practitioners are encouraged to be creative in its use and adapt it to suit the precise task in hand. For example, when assessing a subject who is adamant that his victim cooperated without any pressure, unnecessary initial resistance may be encountered by the use of heading (2.4), 'abuser's overcoming of victim resistance'. It may be more astute to use a more passive phrase at this stage (eg 'how the abuse occurred') in the hope that this will elicit information that may eventually be used to challenge any rationalisations being used by the abuser.

Many pieces of information appear to fit into more than one category and energy should not be wasted worrying about this - it is likely that the different headings will elicit different interpretations.

The format is not intended as a checklist, but more a guide to the type of information that might be elicited and how it might be ordered. It will not provide the definitive guide to what factors are relevant, nor will it produce an assessment of risk on its own. One of its clear strengths is that it encourages practitioners to interpret information in the light of the knowledge base relating to sexually abusive behaviour and thus provides a basis from which professional judgements can be made.

Given the frequency with which this type of format is used by practitioners in field work settings, it is felt appropriate to examine its application in some detail, although what follows is essentially descriptive and should not be viewed as a blueprint for the assessment of risk!

1.0 Basic information

1.1 known abusive behaviour

A resume of current and any previous child protection concerns, whether allegations or accepted abuse, should provide a clear outline of the nature of the issues that must be addressed in identifying and assessing risk.

Most practitioners approach this task by seeking to elicit 'the story of the abuse' from the subject of assessment and then supplement this with any statements to the police that are available (from abuser, victims, partners etc). Often this can result in a 'compare and contrast' type of exercise with at least two perspectives on what exactly happened being generated.

Methods for ordering such information include:

Priestly & McGuire's (1985) '5WH' model
This suggests five headings for consideration when assessing offending behaviour:

1. Who (abused who)?
2. What happened?
3. Where did it happen?
4. When and over what period of time did it happen?
5. Why did it happen?
6. How did the abuse occur?

It should be noted that at this stage the most accurate description of events is the priority aim, and that, although many subjects will say that they most of all want to establish 'why' they behaved in the way they did, this is unlikely to prove a productive line of enquiry at this point. Such a stated aim by a subject is often an attempt to deflect responsibility for the abuse away from what is often the brutally honest single response to such a question: 'because you enjoyed it'.

A variation on the Probation Service's standby of 'ABC'
(Antecedents, Behaviour, Consequences):

1. The build-up to the abuse (both immediate and longer term)
2. A detailed account of the abusive behaviour
3. What happened afterwards and the consequences for all involved.

This method has the advantage that later it can be expanded to consider factors other than behaviour under main headings such as 'thoughts', 'feelings', and 'fantasies' (see Lazarus, 1976, on 'Multi Modal Analysis').

1.2 Offending history

As already indicated, details of previous criminal convictions can provide a good insight into patterns of problematic behaviour towards others and indicate a situation of possible seriousness. Previous convictions for sexual offences should always alert practitioners to the fact that there may be a heightened risk of further abusive behaviour which must be taken seriously and properly assessed. Other offences, such as for domestic violence, or violence generally, may well be significant in assessing the nature of the risk posed. Lengthy records of other, non-assaultive offences might suggest that a pattern of 'rule breaking' has developed. This may be a factor in assessing the subject's general views of societal norms, and their ability to cooperate with planned and mandated intervention.

Clearly the more extensive and serious a subject's record of previous convictions for sexual and violent offences, the greater the concerns and the more likely it is that an assessment of 'high risk' will be made. Any detailed knowledge of previous offending (probation records, case conference minutes, court reports etc) can add significantly to practitioners ability to understand static variables relating to risk, and may prove decisive in subsequent decision making.

The greater the number of separate victims who have been abused (particularly if there is evidence of cross overs, regarding age, gender, extra/intra familial status of victim), the more likely is an assessment that an abuser's pattern of sexual arousal and linked abusive behaviour is indiscriminate.

Once again, it is relatively easy to assess someone with a significant history of sexual abusive behaviour as presenting a high level of risk! However, absence of such indicators does not necessarily mean that an assessment of 'low risk' can be safely made – it may just mean that we do not have sufficient information. The potential must also be acknowledged for risk to increase over time.

1.3 Personal circumstances / background

Life histories, including abuse (sexual and otherwise), attachments and disruptions, form an important backdrop to assessments, often providing information that is directly related to the concerns being explored and to the subject's potential to cooperate with interventions designed to monitor, change and control behaviour.

The current circumstances of the children and adults involved must obviously be described in initial assessments as these are essential factors in understanding the situation and informing plans to manage it. Many practitioners use genograms to depict and clarify family structure and relationships.

2.0 Analysis of abusive behaviour

2.1 Abuser's sexual motivation to offend

It is unlikely that much information in this area will be

forthcoming for an initial assessment. Most abusers have to be engaged in long term work for a significant period of time before disclosing much about their sexual fantasies, masturbatory practices, use of pornography etc. Nevertheless, in the longer term it may be possible to develop a good knowledge about fantasy repertoires and their significance in identifiable sexual assault cycles. Making links between mood swings, external stressors, fluctuating self esteem and the frequency, pattern and content of masturbatory behaviour can contribute significantly to the efficacy of monitoring arrangements in the future. Management of 'high risk' abusers in the community often involves very close (and intrusive) monitoring of their sexual fantasies and masturbatory behaviour.

Subjects should be asked about their masturbatory practices prior to abusing and whether this included use of pornographic material (and of what sort). Practitioners need to be aware that many readily available images not normally associated with pornography can be used to aid arousal (eg. children in clothing catalogues, holiday snaps etc).

In an assessment that takes place over a period of a number of weeks the ability of the subject to provide information about their sexual motivation is an important clue to their likely response to treatment in the future. Responses must be judged in terms of their relative improvement as well as their absolute honesty. A subject who has previously undertaken work on this area is more likely to provide details of this aspect than someone who has been apprehended for the first time and has much invested in denying any sexual component to the behaviour. If the former was less than forthcoming about this area this would be very concerning, whilst an acknowledgement after a number weeks that the behaviour 'must have been sexually motivated' on the part of the latter may suggest the potential for more progress to be made in the future.

In some cases, subjects will appear completely disinhibited about disclosing the nature and extent of their masturbatory behaviour and seem eager to talk. At this end of the 'honesty continuum' lack of information is unlikely to be much of a problem, but practitioners should explore the value base underlying such disclosures (does this suggest a serious lack of internal inhibitors/awareness of 'the wrongness' of sex with children?). Observation of evident satisfaction at discussing sexual fantasies or even arousal during interview will provide important insights for inclusion within assessment.

Available information about previous abuse or convictions may then legitimately be used to speculate or hypothesise about the current situation. For example, If a subject has offended three times previously against boys aged 6 to 9, then it would be reasonable to suggest that there were clear indications of an established pattern of sexual arousal to this gender and age group, even if there was adamant denial of any sexual interest in children! Of course it would be more difficult to hypothesise about the risk this might pose to children in markedly different age groups.

What may be easier to obtain is information about appropriate sexual behaviour and relationships with others. Long term intervention would certainly involve the taking of a life and sexual history. Any history of abuse should be noted; many abusers have been abused themselves as children (though not necessarily sexually) and these experiences may have influenced their perceptions of what it means to be a victim, their current repertoires of sexual fantasies, their self esteem, confidence etc.

Other people may be able to shed light on an abuser's sexual motivation to offend (victim statements, retrospective comments from nonabusing partner etc) and may provide evidence of distorted emotional closeness or relationships with children. Subjects themselves may be prepared to talk about their relationships with children, even if denying any component of sexual attraction. Such disclosures should be noted, as they are likely to contain significant cognitive distortions that will need to be addressed in the future.

Psychological assessments may provide considerable insights into this particular factor, often supplemented by validated questionnaires (eg the Multiphasic Sex Inventory of Nicols and Mullinder (1984). On occasions, phallometric assessment may be available from use of a penile plethysmograph (in itself a highly specialist skill), but practitioners are warned to be cautious in interpreting findings and must avoid the trap of assuming that they represent an 'objective, scientific' evaluation of a subject's arousal patterns. There are, moreover, considerable reservations about the reliability of such testing and doubts about the ethics of its use.

2.2 Overcoming the abuser's internal inhibitions

If the abuser has taken some responsibility for the abuse, then his views on how he allowed himself to behave in such a way will be informative and provide a benchmark against which to assess progress over time (as, hopefully, intervention will result in increasing honesty). Assessments should seek to establish how an abuser attributes responsibility for the behaviour, and should note distortions that suggest mutuality with the victim. In long term work, efforts should be made to identify the precise nature of the cognitive distortions employed at different stages of the assault cycle. Denial has long been viewed as a significant factor in assessing risk, and whilst absolute denial cannot be said to equate automatically with increased risk, the prognosis for risk management in such situations can hardly be good.

As indicated above, the subject's views on relationships with children will provide vital information about how responsibility for initiating and maintaining 'friendships' is attributed. Own experiences of victimisation may play an important part in understanding the degree of (or more often lack of) empathy towards a victim, which is a key factor in assessing risk and fixing a marker against which to evaluate future progress. Care is needed to spot abusers who appear to have a very well developed appreciation of the negative impact of abuse on victims, as this may provide a key to understanding the nature of their sexual arousal. In such situations you may be dealing with a 'sadistic abuser', for whom the pain and distress of a victim is in itself arousing.

Other factors may be more readily noted, such as external stressors, use of drugs and alcohol and mental health problems. These may have already resulted in statutory intervention and a number of agencies may have relevant information about them. The impact of substance misuse immediately prior to abusing is often overemphasised by abusers (who are often keen to displace responsibility), but recourse to victim statements will often indicate that the abuse was in fact carefully planned and executed - not the behaviour of someone 'out of their head' ! However, such disinhibition may be a more significant factor in masturbatory practice and rehearsal and may have clear implications for future risk management.

The process of assessment may enable practitioners to make some tentative remarks about the subjects level of self esteem, assertiveness, social and problem solving skills and the degree to which masturbatory fantasy and sexually abusive behaviour constituted a 'retreat' from problems being experienced.

2.3 Circumventing external inhibitors

Moving to the last two of Finkelhor's factors (see pp 27-29), information is generally more readily available from others (adults, victims, siblings), and less will depend on the abuser's degree of cooperation with the assessment process.

Knowledge of how the abuser manipulated (or groomed) the environment is of course crucial to an understanding of the methods used to set up situations where abuse could occur. This should inform the setting up of monitoring arrangements for the future. The nature of relationships between adults with responsibility for the children requires exploration, there should be particular concern if there is evidence of domestic violence. The ability of the nonabusing partner to manage risk is a key consideration when family reunification is being considered and thus the power dynamics operant between partners while the abuse was occurring will be an important factor to consider.

Evidence that other responsible adults knew that abuse was occurring but were unable to intervene, or chose not to, must be viewed with extreme seriousness and appropriate intervention decided upon.

2.4 Overcoming victim resistance

Information about the development of an abusive relationship with a victim is vital, and initially is likely to be mainly obtained from victim statements, video interviews and retrospective comments from others (family and professionals). Evidence of patterned behaviour and an ability to notice and target vulnerability will be useful in predicting future risk and a detailed knowledge of the process of abusing will help in understanding the impact on the victim. Children exposed to threat and violence are likely to have experienced severe trauma and disempowerment whilst children bribed with treats and affection are more likely to struggle with feelings of guilt and responsibility. In some situations alcohol or drugs may have been used to entice potential victims (the thrill of the forbidden) and/or reduce their ability to resist sexual advances. Such practices can leave victims feelings particularly responsible for the subsequent abuse and reluctant to tell others who might have intervened.

Suggestions or threats to maintain secrecy following abuse should be noted, suggesting the development of a pattern of manipulative and controlling behaviour.

An abuser's account of the abuse must be noted, whilst acknowledging that in the early stages this will almost certainly be awash with distortion, denial and rationalisation. As already noted, part of the job of assessment is to place markers against which later progress (or its absence) can be judged. Of course a subject who denies absolutely will have little to say in this area, but can be asked to account for any statements / video interviews undertaken by the child.

If a degree of responsibility is being accepted, questions should be asked about how the abuser thinks the victim will have experienced the abusive behaviour. This should reveal more distortions that will have to be addressed in longer term 'victim empathy work' and give clues to likely ability in the future to take account of the needs of others (and particularly children).

3.0 Analysis of current circumstances

3.1 Abuser's current sexual motivations

It is likely that in the period immediately following allegations or apprehension, arousal to inappropriate stimuli may be temporary inhibited through anxiety and that in consequence accurate assessment may be particularly difficult. Even if the subject is prepared to discuss this area of his life, in initial interviews it is likely that you will be told of a complete cessation of masturbation with any sexual fantasies being confined solely to those involving consenting adults. Even if this information was accurate at that time, assessment could not assume that this would continue longer term – and in fact the knowledge base suggests that the opposite may well be more likely.

Longer term assessments would seek to chart changes in fantasy repertoires over time, the frequency of masturbation and changes in the profile of sexual preferences. The use of 'pie charts' to allow diagrammatic representation of changes from one assessment to another can be particularly useful. The results of an abuser's attempts to control arousal to inappropriate fantasy should be recorded and an attempt made to see how fluctuating success might be linked to other aspects of his life and circumstances (in particular in relation to any stressors identified in 2.2). However, this is demanding and challenging work, and most practitioners have to rely almost solely on the self report of the abuser to gain a picture of this normally very private behaviour. Fantasy modification programmes are possible, but the first priority of such intervention must be to monitor and control sexual arousal rather than relying on attempts at change. Indeed, a very significant change is often that an abuser begins to accept the need for such intrusive exercises.

Again, information may be more readily available about appropriate sexual relationships that the abuser may currently be involved in, although dilemmas will be raised about others' right to confidentiality. The fact that an abuser may now appear to have a perfectly satisfactory relationship with a consenting adult should not result in the assumption that there is no longer any risk to children. Many sexual abusers of children are able to be involved in sexual relationships with adults at the same time.

3.2 Abuser's maintenance of internal controls

A crucial factor is the assessment of the degree of responsibility that the abuser is taking for the abuse and the closeness of his version of events with that of his victim. Of course, discrepancies can either be indicative of serious concerns, or be insignificant differences. By and large victim statements are viewed as likely to be more accurate than those of abusers.

An abuser's degree of insight into his abusive behaviour as a process (see chapter 2) is an important matter for evaluation. Those who are aware of the steps that they took that eventually resulted in abuse (or maintained an abusive situation) should be better prepared to tackle growing risk in the future. Although 'insight is insufficient on its own for change', its presence alongside motivation is vital.

The abuser's ability to empathise with what his victim has experienced (is continuing to experience and is likely to experience in the future) will provide further indicators of current levels of cognitive distortions, but 'victim empathy' is a particularly difficult issue in work with sexual abusers, and it is relatively easy to 'talk the talk' without any underlying changes in attitudes and views occurring. Abusers may typically exhibit considerable distress about 'what they have done', but care is required to analyse this as it frequently relates more to their predicament and losses than to concern for the impact of their behaviour upon a victim (see chapter 3).

The ability to empathise with others has, at its root, an ability to 'be in touch' with ones own feelings. Many sexual abusers of children (and indeed men in general) struggle to name and acknowledge emotions and have little understanding of how thoughts and feelings can relate to actions. It may be that some remedial work is necessary in this area and, if so, it should be clearly stated that this is the case. Other abusers may lack very basic knowledge about sex education, gender dynamics and what constitutes the age of consent for sexual relationships. Such deficits must also be addressed in any subsequent programme of intervention.

Where gross denial constitutes a sticking point, some thought might be given to what is encouraging continued distortions and what the subject might have to lose by greater honesty. This will inform the prognosis for increasing honesty in the future and provide pointers for how to tackle and shift the blocks. Persistent and rigid cognitive distortions may indicate likely resistance to the changes necessary if safe management of risk is to succeed. Changing abusers' rationalisations and minimisations is a key task if attempts to strengthen their motivation and ability to rebuild and maintain internal inhibitors to re-abuse are to be successful.

The motivation and ability of the abuser to manage future risk should be addressed. To what extent does the abuser acknowledge and understand the risk that he may pose in the future? How prepared is the abuser to consider risky situations and rehearse avoidance strategies? What is an abuser's ability to prioritise the needs of children above others and their own? Assessments of self esteem and self confidence will have a bearing on how realistic it is for the abuser to cooperate with programmes designed to manage risk. This is typically a very daunting task, with much pain and difficulty to be lived with if it is to be successful. It is not unusual for abusers to become demotivated by anger when the enormity of their task becomes overwhelming and for carefully constructed avoidance strategies to be swept away with thoughts like 'why shouldn't I fantasise about that child ?' ... 'I deserve some fun and excitement' ... 'I'm fed up always having to monitor what I think, feel etc ....'

As concerning as self esteem deficits are instances of very high and unrealistic self confidence. Abusers with 'omnipotent' personalities can be extremely difficult to engage with and the prognosis for change and control is often very poor.

Current stressors in an abuser's life and how they are being managed should be considered, with particular attention given to control over the use of disinhibitors (particularly substance abuse identified in 2.2.)

Where there is a history of mental health problems a psychiatric assessment will be required and where learning difficulties are known or suspected a psychological assessment of cognitive functioning should be sought.

3.3 Maintenance of external controls over the abuser

The identification of potentially risky situations will clearly help to plan a risk management strategy, and subjects should be encouraged to speculate about these. Longer term work would seek to analyse these in detail and encourage the abuser to develop credible avoidance strategies. However, in the immediate term, attention must be focused on whether it is possible for the abuser to avoid contact with potential victims and / or be safely supervised in this by other responsible adults.

The attitude and understanding of non abusing partners is

critical in considering the safety of children in family situations. Assessment should seek to discover the extent to which the victim's version of events is believed; how a partner attributes responsibility for previous abuse; and the extent to which there is acceptance of a future risk, and motivation to cooperate in its management. Contextual details are important: the nature of relationships within the family and the various power dynamics, and the ability of the partner to act independently in the interests of child protection. (Pithers, 1990, found a powerful link between relationship difficulties and relapse.) Personal difficulties (health problems, mental health problems, substance misuse) may well have a bearing on a partners ability to adequately protect their children in what can be the most trying of circumstances.

Note: It should be acknowledged that non abusing partners may well take a considerable time to assimilate what has happened, and may therefore present initially as being in gross denial when in fact they may be in a state of shock. A good indicator of a partners motivation to cooperate with statutory agencies may be her involvement in the assessment process and any progress she may have made in this during its short time. A shift from absolute denial and resistance to acceptance of the need for statutory intervention, however grudgingly, may be all that can be expected over the course of a few weeks. Written agreements should be used to formalise such gains and to spell out precisely the task of child protection that is being required.

There may be other responsible adults who are in regular contact with the children (grandparents, aunts and uncles, friends etc) and their attitudes and understanding should also be assessed. How aware and accepting of risk are they? Are they in a position to provide support to the victim and nonabusing partner? Are they prepared to take part in any monitoring arrangements?

Any monitoring will be set up and coordinated by statutory agencies/professional networks and it is important that such plans are detailed and shown to be workable. The abuser's ability to cooperate with proposed monitoring arrangements will be central to any assessment of risk management and much may be deduced from attitudes during the process of assessment. Is there an acceptance of the need for intervention? Is there potential for positive change to occur over time?

3.4 Abuser's contact with potential victims

Contact with children who are of the same gender and similar age to known previous victim(s) will be a cause for particular concern. However, contact with a child of a different age or gender cannot necessarily be assumed to represent a low risk.

If contact is proposed (or simply continuing) between the subject and the child who has been victimised, the impact on the child must be carefully assessed. What are the child's views on what has happened and what should happen now? Are there conflicts between what a victim says she wishes to occur and what is in her best interests? What potential does the victim have to protect him/herself in the face of further abuse and what work needs to be undertaken to develop this? Given current understanding of the concept of 'grooming', assessing what is in the child's best interest, disentangled from the interests of the adults involved, can be particularly problematic.

In a family, it is likely that the victim will have siblings and assessments of risk will be required for these and indeed for any other children with whom the subject has regular contact. The attitude of the parents of these children will also have to be included in the wider assessment.

4.0 Conclusions and assessment of risk

Having gone through the process of assessment and ordered the information, conclusions must be drawn and judgements made. This is best viewed as a process in which the knowledge gained is reviewed and evaluated.

Absences of information in areas felt to be important is commonplace (particularly at initial assessment stage) and should not prevent an assessment from being completed – indeed observations about this form a vital part of the overall analysis. Any gaps in knowledge should be highlighted for consideration in subsequent intervention.

Key factors identified should be assessed in the light of the current professional knowledge base about sexual abusers (including base rates for recidivism), taking care to distinguish fact from interpretation/hypothesis. Reasons should be given for conclusions drawn. Managing the relationship between factors identified as significant in a specific case and the backdrop of the knowledge base is crucial in arriving at sound and defensible judgements. Moore (1997) cautions that care is needed lest the knowledge base and clinical experience are allowed to drive the assessment in the face of the known facts about the case.

Similarly, worrying aspects of a particular situation should not be evaluated without reference to the knowledge base. As in work with sexual abusers in general, practitioners must ensure they adopt a balanced approach which works *with* the tensions involved rather than *in spite of* them. 'Maintaining an open mind' is a skill well known to child protection workers and it should be exercised throughout the (possibly lengthy) process of evaluating all the notes made in the format, highlighting those thought most pertinent and then drawing these points together to give an overall assessment which is based on the information available.

The drawing of conclusions might involve the following process (see also report outline in chapter 7):

- Consideration of information gathered and ordered within a multifactor format
- Identification of key factors that would inform an assessment of risk. Patterns of behaviour should be isolated, although particular care is required to avoid 'forcing' disparate incidents to conform to a pattern of concerns.
- Conclusions drawn about the nature, extent and generalisability of the risk posed. What is the likelihood of abusive behaviour in the future? How is it likely to manifest itself and through what processes? Who is at risk, in what circumstances and to what likely effect?
- Conclusions about risk management in the light of the above. What are the key elements to be considered in assessing the potential for this risk to be managed? To what extent can specified risky situations be safely monitored and by whom? What are the safeguards? Are they sufficient? How likely are they to breakdown?
- Overall conclusions and judgements must be made as to whether the proposed circumstances have the potential to be managed safely. In doing this, practitioners should take care

to give their view of the integrity of the assessment, clearly stating any limitations resulting from lack of relevant information, professional expertise etc. Alternative understandings of the information gathered must be noted, with comments made about their relative accuracy, usefulness etc. Most assessments will comprise a mixture of opinion based on validated knowledge (official statistics, research findings etc) and hypothesis based on clinical experience and it should be clear which is which.

- Issues for further assessment should be identified, with recommendations for specialist input if appropriate.
- Risk management plans should be detailed and specific, and if subsequently adopted, should form part of a written agreement between the adults in a family and statutory agencies.
- The response of the subjects to the completed assessment should be included, with comments on how this might inform perceptions of the manageability of risk.

Generating conclusions in order to complete a risk assessment process is typically very demanding and once again practitioners are advised to maintain a 'balanced approach' in commenting on circumstances which are often emotive and anxiety provoking. Briggs et al (1997, p146) warn against over estimations of risk.

Risk assessment is an area notoriously fraught with subjective evaluations and a common error is that of making false positive judgements i.e. assuming clients or individuals to be at greater risk, or riskier than is actually the case.

On the other hand a number of public enquiries into child abuse in the UK have identified 'unrealistic optimism' about families on the part of child protection workers, which highlights the danger of overestimating the potential for adults to manage the risk of sexually abusive behaviour within family situations.

Making judgements about other people that will have a significant impact on their lives is without doubt a daunting task and the fear of making a mistake can be disempowering. However, this pressure can be managed through co-working and supervision (see chapter 7), and by providing assessments that detail clearly how you came to your conclusions. Decisions at conference, for example, can be genuinely shared by providing participants with a clear account of the assessment, which would allow others to either own or challenge findings.

Undertaking assessments in such a structured, yet flexible manner can give practitioners a methodology which is supportive and rigorous without being unduly prescriptive. Co-workers can share information and ideas within a common framework which invites abusers and their families to consider the key components of their situation and which gives them the opportunity to take responsibility for beginning to address them.

Chapter 6

Assessment of risk: Examples

THIS CHAPTER sets out to provide a comparative study of circumstances not uncommon when assessing risk in family situations (see also chapter 3). Two family scenarios are explored in four stages utilising the overall framework suggested in chapter 5, with each section of information followed by a discussion of key issues.

The exercise is essentially descriptive in that its aim is limited to that of providing a flavour of assessment. Obviously any assessment in the real world will be far more complicated than is portrayed here and all situations requiring assessment will be unique. What follows is not a blueprint for other, real assessments, but an adaptation of a commonly used training tool.

1. Basic information

Scenario one

The subject of assessment is 40 years old, white. He is a successful businessman, married for 20 years (wife of same age) with 2 girls aged 13 and 15.

The 15 year old girl had alleged that her father had 'come on to her', climbing into her bed 'to give her a hug' having just come home late from a party. He had kissed her, rubbed her breasts and attempted to put his hand between her legs before she pushed him away and he stopped.

She had telephoned the police the following morning and he had cooperated fully in interview, breaking down in tears saying that he was so ashamed of what he had done. He acknowledged having 'a bit of an erection' but says he had drunk too much 'for much more'. He says that he had smoked a joint for the first time in years at the party and feels that his usual night time hug 'got out of hand and that he 'just forgot himself'. When she had pushed at his chest he 'come to his senses' and stopped immediately and apologised before going to his own bed.

He had no previous criminal convictions.

He was processed through the criminal justice system and was sentenced to 6 months imprisonment despite a PSR recommendation for a Probation Order. He is to be released in 4 weeks time and says he intends to move home.

Scenario two

This subject is also 40 years old and white. He has a history of institutionalisation (care, prison) and alternates employment as a labourer on short term contracts with periods of unemployment. He is due to be released from prison (Social Security Fraud – 2 years imprisonment) and wishes to return home to his wife (aged 30), stepson (15) and stepdaughter aged 13.

Previous convictions include:

- (20) – Unlawful Sexual Intercourse, against his 15 year old girlfriend, who had become pregnant.
- (25) – Actual Bodily Harm on 17 year old female partner, after she had 'flirted with someone else'.
- (30) – Indecent Assault and Gross Indecency – He had worked at a Games Workshop in town, where many boys and young men met to play with the shop displays and buy models. He had invited two 10 year old boys home to play with his armies. He had admitted mutual masturbation on 'a number of occasions' over a six month period and was sentenced to 18 months imprisonment. He had undertaken 'treatment' in prison in an experimental group work programme run by psychologists and probation officers.

Discussion: Initial views on risk

The clear difference between the two scenarios is that of previous criminal convictions; the man in scenario 1 has none, whilst the man in scenario 2 has a significant record up to 10 years ago which included sexual offences against three individuals (2 boys, 1 girl) and an offence of violence against an adult woman.

There is, therefore, much more information available on the scenario 2 man about past problematic behaviour. He has offended against both genders and the offences against the boys suggest considerable planning and preparation. His assertion that the offence of Unlawful Sexual Intercourse did not involve any coercion will be difficult to check out and will have to be assessed in the light of his subsequent assault on a young woman five years later. It is likely, given these static variables that this man will be viewed as 'high risk' (the Fisher/Thornton algorithm gives a score of 4, i.e. 'high + risk').

Moreover, the man in scenario 2 has been living with his stepson for five years and will have therefore joined this family when this boy would have been the same age as his previous male victims. Nevertheless, there have been no concerns brought to the attention of statutory agencies during this period and it will be noted that his last conviction for a sexual offence was 10 years ago.

The relative lack of information regarding the man in scenario 1 creates considerable problems for the assessor. His lack of any previous convictions and the fact that statutory agencies are not aware of any previous concerns in the family are likely to generate an initial view of his risk as being 'low' (the Fisher/Thornton algorithm gives a score of 0, i.e. 'low risk').

However, the fact that the problematic behaviour of the man in scenario 1 is very recent and that his victim will continue to live in the house following his proposed return is a matter of concern. Assessors need not only to consider the risk of further sexually abusive acts, but also the impact on his daughter of living in close proximity to her abuser. It is likely, in these circumstances, that the initial view of risk might be amended to 'low-medium'.

2. Assessment of known abusive behaviour

Scenario one

The subject reluctantly concedes that he must have been 'a bit aroused' to do what he did, but denies this is anything but a one off. He is adamant that he had not found his daughter attractive prior to the incident, although he volunteers that he has been aware of her 'developing body' in the last year or so.

She had told the police that she now remembered a 'funny cuddle' a couple of months ago when her dad had got 'a bit breathless', but she hadn't thought much about it at the time.

He views the combination of drink, a joint at a party and his 'weakness' to be causal factors, 'I got carried away ... I shouldn't have'.

He always gives his daughter a hug on going to bed and sometimes they get in each other's beds for 'a cuddle'. He says that this has been regular behaviour since the children were very small. This is confirmed by his wife, who says that there is nothing wrong with being physically close, 'we are ... or were ... a very affectionate family'.

He gives an opinion that his daughter had been as involved as him in the instigation of sexual behaviour, 'backing' into him and causing further arousal. He says that she has told him that she was half asleep and had had a drink herself earlier that evening.

Scenario two

The subject acknowledges that he can become aroused to boys 9-15 years old and that in the past used child pornography to masturbate 3-4 times per day. Admits abuse of the 2 boys on numerous occasions.

At the time he felt he wasn't doing any harm. He had been abused as a child and had not been hurt. Used amphetamine when masturbating/fantasising, but never with the boys.

He acknowledged that he had worked at the shop because he liked the company of young boys and had got to know the two boys he eventually abused very well. His invitations to them to visit his home had not been secretive, he had spoken to both boys parents and obtained their consent.

He had provided fun afternoons, with lots of pop and cakes, frequent water fights and wrestling competitions. At the time he had let himself believe that the sexual activity had 'grown out of the messing about' but now knows different.

Discussion

Differences in the quality of information available continues to have a significant impact on the assessors' ability to make sense of the nature and extent of the potential risk facing both families.

The man in scenario 2 has confirmed the level of concern previously expressed and the likelihood is that his actions in the past represented a pattern of sexually abusive behaviour. He has furnished information that his offences against pre-pubescent boys were planned and accompanied by considerable use of masturbatory fantasy. He had rationalised his action by reference to experiences of his own abuse as a boy and his victim's responses, which he had viewed as very positive. It is likely that views on risk are likely to remain unchanged (i.e. 'high').

However, assessors are likely to feel some reassurance that the man in scenario 2 is responding in an apparently open and honest manner and the indications are that the previous group work programme has had a positive impact.

With regard to the man in scenario 1, assessors are likely to struggle to gain a clearer picture of the nature and extent of the sexually abuse behaviour. The incident leading to conviction is still presented as a 'one off', perpetrated in unusual circumstances (he was drunk and stoned) but in a context of general physical closeness where cuddles in bed were a frequent occurrence for all family members. There are also hints that his sexual arousal to his daughter may have pre-dated the incident which is acknowledged, however neither father or daughter have been prepared to talk further about such a possibility. Assessors will be alarmed about his remarks about his daughter's, at least partial, active involvement in the abuse, and his pointing out that she was herself somewhat disinhibited through drink. These views undermine his constant statements to the effect that he has done wrong and is entirely responsible for what happened.

Despite these worries and apparent loose ends, it is unlikely that assessors would shift their initial view of 'low-medium' risk, but anxiety may well be mounting that significant pieces of information may be being withheld.

3. Assessment of current and proposed future circumstances

Scenario one

The subject says he is currently sexually inactive ('this has scared me off sex'). He views his 20 years of marriage as demonstrating that he is not 'a deviant'. His wife refuses to discuss 'intimate details'.

He says he's been under tremendous stress since 'all this' (going to prison, letting his wife down and not being able to help with the children, both of whom are being very difficult). He has no intention of ever smoking a joint again.

He has stated his intention to work with social workers but frequently loses his temper – he is viewed as being difficult to work with. His wife has come to relate to workers with a cold fury and is outraged that they are not being supported in trying to put the family back together again. She feels much more damage has occurred since her husband's arrest than through his prior behaviour. She says that there will be no repetition.

His 15 year old daughter says that she wants him home and is confident that she can deal with this – 'he'll not dare do anything again', 'that's why I phoned the police'. She rows regularly with her mother and is missing school on a regular basis (which pre-dated the incident). She has considered, and refused an offer of therapy (after a discussion with her mother).

Their 13 year old son has become quiet and watchful and became upset when his dad's conviction was alluded to, shouting out 'its not true'. He is angry that his father is not at home. School have no worries, he remains a very hard worker.

Scenario two

The subject reports that occasionally fantasies of boys intrude when he is having sex with his wife or masturbating but that he is successful at using 'switching techniques' learnt in the group. He has occasionally used adult female pornography (magazines) in the recent past but hasn't used child pornography 'for years'. He says that he has never found his stepson attractive and wouldn't have moved in with the family if he had.

He drinks alcohol to excess sometimes but uses no illegal drugs. Says he has learnt that sex with boys is wrong and has no intention of allowing himself to abuse again – he is not interested and has too much to lose.

Despite initial irritation at 'having to go through all this again' he has cooperated well with his current supervising officer and worked through reports from his groupwork 10 years previously (which had been cautiously optimistic). His current partner knew about his previous convictions and has indicated that she understands he presents a risk. However, she says he has demonstrated over the last 5 years his worth and she feels her children are not at risk – although she would report any concerns.

His stepchildren are enthusiastic about his return home and say he has never tried to do anything sexual with them and they would stop him if he did. Their mother had told them about his past and the bad things he had done to children. They had voted on whether he should move in. Both children say that he gets on very well with their mother, and 'makes her happy'.

The man states that there have been no 'risky situations' since moving in with the family and he can't think of any that might arise. When pushed he felt that perhaps difficulties between himself and his wife might generate tensions but he couldn't honestly see that resulting in him abusing again.

Discussion

The man in scenario 2 appears to be able to acknowledge that sexual arousal to pre-pubescent boys remains an issue for him, if much reduced from previous years. There is further evidence of his ability to retain and utilise insights and techniques from his previous 'treatment' and a willingness to cooperate with assessment and future monitoring. He no longer appears to disinhibit himself in the same way we used when previously offending.

Other family members in scenario 2 seem to have been provided with considerable information about his previous offending and thus empowered to protect themselves. His wife feels that his risk is much diminished and is credible in stating that any problems would be shared with her, and thus passed onto the relevant authorities. There is no evidence that either child has been abused, but while the stepson has 'grown out of' the apparent previous target age range for boys, his stepdaughter is now 'growing into' the target age range for girls.

It is unlikely that an assessor would suggest that the original label of 'high risk' should be moderated, but the response of all family members indicates that the potential for its safe management may be good.

The relationship between the assessors and the family in scenario 1 appears, unfortunately, to be further deteriorating, as they resent continued intervention and being prevented (as they see it) from 'getting on with their lives'. Very little information has been elicited regarding current sexual practices/motivations and little progress made regarding the accepting of full responsibility for the abuse (apart from the oft repeated 'I take full responsibility ... now leave us be to sort the mess out'). Current stressors are viewed as relating almost entirely to statutory intervention rather than being integral to family functioning and it is therefore difficult to isolate and discuss potentially risk situations in the future.

Hopes that his wife might effectively monitor the situation must be tempered by her resistance to official intervention and her apparent impact on her daughter's decision not to accept counselling. Her daughter's stance also presents problems, for whilst her confidence in being able to deal with the return of her father is evidenced by her telephoning the police following the original incident, assessors are likely to remain concerned that she has not been able to 'work through' the implications of her abuse, that there are considerable tensions between her and her mother and that she has problems in other areas of her life.

Although there is no evidence that their son has been abused, or that the father has any sexual interest in boys, his response to the situation is obviously a matter of concern. Of course, his withdrawal and outburst when questioned may simply be the frightened response of a young person caught up in a family in crisis.

Assessors are likely to be left feeling concerned about the family's potential to manage the proposed rehabilitation of the father, given the apparent degree of shared minimisations and rationalisations. However, the degree of risk actually posed remains unclear and there is little hard evidence to suggest that earlier conceptions of 'low-medium' should be modified.

4. Conclusions for the two scenarios

Scenario 1

Assessment has been difficult in scenario 1, because despite the apparent lack of previous incidents, the knowledge base would suggest that it is likely that there were preceding behaviours (fantasies, masturbation and possibly incidents). There have been hints that this may have been the case, but there is information relating to one incident only, and the family remain adamant that this was atypical behaviour which will not be repeated.

Despite an initial readiness to cooperate, members of the family have become more resistant to the process of assessment as it has become obvious that neither their view of what has happened nor their prognosis for the future will necessarily be accepted. Assessors will have concerns as the father is failing to take full responsibility for the abuse and as both parents now seem unwilling to acknowledge and act upon the potential risk posed for the future. They state that the man no longer has access to his daughter's bed and that all family members are avoiding walking around in the nude, so there will be no risky situations in the future.

The daughter appears to be capable of rebuffing any further advances by her father, but the full impact of the abuse upon her is difficult to gauge. However, her relationship difficulties at home and poor school attendance are a matter of concern and require analysis and attention.

The couple's other child also appears to be struggling, but there is no evidence that he has been abused, or is at risk. It is likely that his difficulties reflect the general family tensions at this time, and he does appear to have school as a refuge.

Assessors in this situation are likely to feel that they need further information (some of which might have been deliberately withheld from them) before reaching any conclusions. However, this may be the best that can be managed, given the short timescale and the poor relationship between family and professionals. Judgements will have to be made on the information available.

Assessors will need to take care that their worries about non-cooperation and resistance do not falsely elevate perceptions of risk significantly beyond that indicated by known static variables. The most likely hypothesis would be that there had been a number of incidents over a period of at least 3-6 months, and that his behaviour had escalated in its intrusiveness over this time. Even this would not alter the Fisher/Thornton evaluation of risk as being 'low' and assessor anxiety has already modified this to 'low-medium'! There is no evidence of other victims.

His daughter is nearly 16 and has stated categorically that she wants him home and knows that her experience of informing the authorities had at least stopped any sexual abuse from continuing.

It is unlikely that assessment of this situation would suggest that the risk of further abuse was so high that rehabilitation was out of the question. Indeed, it is more likely that rehabilitation would be linked to an agreed plan that could be monitored and assessed over time. The following recommendations might well be made:

- The father not to return directly home, but to live with his brother while gradual rehabilitation takes place.
- Hence, decisions must be made about an agreed timescale, contact arrangements, and means of monitoring and assessing the process.
- Work to be undertaken with both children to ensure they are both best able to protect themselves (clarifying which behaviours are OK/NOT OK, who they would tell etc).
- Work to be undertaken with both parents to explain professional concerns about risk and the need to reduce any continuing harm to their daughter from her experiences.

- Efforts be undertaken to air and resolve tensions between mother and daughter.
- Action required to address poor school attendance.

(One could speculate as to how different the outcome of the assessment might be if the couple's youngest child was a 13 year old girl, and the oldest girl was running away from home on a regular basis).

Scenario 2

In contrast, the assessment process in scenario 2 has been relatively straightforward, with all family members cooperating fully and enabling a wide range of relevant information to be gathered. There is no doubt that this man's known previous behaviour suggests that he is 'high risk', the evidence is consistent with the knowledge base, despite the gap of 10 years since his last conviction for a sexual offence. Assessors should be wary of reducing their concept of risk significantly below that indicated by static variables on the basis of the family's positive response to assessment. Many assessors would want this situation to be manageable but should remember that this assessment has already been moderated from Fisher &Thornton's categorisation of 'high +' to 'high' risk.

Assessors will undoubtedly be concerned about the stepson and the risk that he was abused when the man entered the family. They will also be very aware that had an assessment been undertaken at that time it is unlikely that the man's moving in would have been sanctioned. However, there is no evidence that this has happened and indeed both children seem appropriately aware of their stepfather's past and confident of their ability to handle any difficulties in the future. Similarly, mother is well informed and has indicated that she would have no hesitation in dealing with any abusive behaviour.

Although the man has benefited from his groupwork programme 10 years previously, it will be of some concern that he is unable to think of any specific risky situations against which he should guard. He states that he has never had intimate care of the children. The stability and apparent 'safeness' of the current situation should not allow the implications of the original 'high risk' analysis to fade. Work is needed to maintain safe management of risk if, as is likely, a return home is agreed.

In this event the following recommendations might be made:

- Close monitoring and assessment of his return home.
- Work with both adults to review comprehensively work undertaken 10 years previously, and to update their understanding of 'risk' and 'risk management'.
- Work with both children, in particular the girl, to ensure that they are best placed to protect themselves and have access to others outside of the family.
- Counselling to be offered regarding the man's own abuse.

(It would be interesting to consider how this assessment might be different if the assessors had met more resistance from the family, or if the stepson's response had been less reassuring, or if there had been a 5 year old boy in the family.)

Final observations

Those interested might wish to order the information provided in their own version of the format, identifying key issues, relationships between factors, gaps in knowledge etc. Do you agree with the comments that have been made in relation to assessment? Justify any differences that you might have. Would they result in actions different to those alluded to here?

As trainers we are aware of the helpfulness of a comparative exercise. Different aspects and types of information can be explored within the space defined by the two scenarios and people feel reassured that there are going to be more 'relative' than 'absolute' judgements. Real assessments tend to come along on their own and real, absolute decisions need to be made on the basis of their findings. Practitioners who can develop experience of assessments over time are better able to locate types and degrees of issues within an informed context, which should reduce the risk of over reaction on the one hand and insufficient action on the other.

Chapter 7

Assessment processes

THE PREVIOUS three chapters have concentrated on what information is required in order to produce a useful risk assessment, and how it might be interpreted. This chapter focuses on how relevant information may be gathered and the human dynamics that must be managed to do so effectively.

Risk assessment is at its best a process in which information acquired from written and official sources is combined with knowledge gained from interaction with an abuser (or alleged abuser), non-abusing partner and children in the family. If the professional is lucky, such assessment takes place in the context of a longer term professional relationship with the abuser in which contracting, motivational work and some offence focused work has already occurred. Denial and resistance should have been acknowledged as likely to be operant during the sessions, making it easier to cite areas of concern while maintaining a working relationship.

More often, risk assessments are required in very different, highly fraught circumstances, and within tight time limits due to legal and procedural imperatives. Most practitioners will not need to be told that it is then difficult to build up a good working relationship and thus to obtain sufficient or accurate information – a process essential if adequate assessments are to be made. Denial and resistance to engagement in the process of assessment will often prove powerful frustrators of analysis.

In order to avoid lengthy repetition of cumbersome phrases, this chapter will refer to any adults in the assessment process as 'subjects' (primarily an abuser/alleged abuser and non-abusing partner).

The context within which assessments of risk take place

If risk assessment is in itself a challenging activity, the complications created by the context in which it is generally undertaken creates more pressures - and without doubt, pitfalls. Although not as litigious (yet?) as the USA, our society is critical of poor professional practice, including assessments which in retrospect were clearly inadequate/dangerous and resulted in a well publicised creation of a further victim.

There is an expectation that obvious risk must be properly and safely managed, and whilst few professionals would disagree with such sentiments, what is 'obvious' in hindsight was often less clear at the point of assessment. We would reiterate that risk assessments can be at best only partial attempts to predict future behaviour within limited circumstances. Nevertheless popular concerns are increasingly risk orientated, with high expectations on 'those responsible'. Martin Woollacott (1997) suggests that ' as we become more adept at forecasting at least some risk we become more and more preoccupied by it, and more demanding that government take responsibility for managing risk' (as welfare and criminal justice agencies have become only too aware—see Douglas, 1992). Morrison (1997) goes further, talking of blaming systems that are 'ready to treat every death as chargeable to someone's account, every accident as caused by someone's criminal negligence, and every sickness a threatened prosecution'.

If there are high public expectations about the management of risk in general, there are very powerful additional tensions in the area of sexually abusive behaviour. Societal ambivalence about sexual abuse, on the one hand demonising identified abusers, while on the other, denying the extent and nature of sexual violence (see Gocke, 1991; 1995), creates a very emotional but ill informed climate for public discourse. The professional response to these factors is circumscribed by a poor legal and procedural reality. The overwhelming majority of sexually abusive acts committed in our society do not result in prosecution and thus many attempts at risk management are hampered by a lack of legal sanction that often distorts the balancing of children's needs with those of adults. The well publicised resource shortfalls in probation and social service departments merely compound the difficulties in providing an adequate service in this area.

In these circumstances the pressures on managers and workers are immense and it is not surprising that the demand for 'certainty' in prediction is commonplace when decisions need to be made about the future of children and families. Certainty of course is unlikely to be found in an assessment of sexually abusive behaviour - which of itself must be viewed as a risky activity. A more acceptable yardstick in auditing the quality of assessment and subsequent action maybe the notion of 'defensible decision making' - that assessment was thorough and well informed and that in the light of the information thus generated, the decisions made were the best that could be made at the time. Whilst this may retain a flavour of 'back covering, the advantages that can accrue by clearly laying out the basis for assessing risk in any particular circumstances in the protecting of others, may also coincide with professionals' legitimate need to protect themselves! The notion of 'evidence based social work' fits well with the production of competent risk assessments.

Nevertheless, no matter how well trained, experienced and knowledgeable, it is difficult for practitioners to avoid defensiveness when assessing risk. Fear of 'getting it wrong' can be particularly disempowering and can often result in a failure to deliver any form of assessment. Practitioners are well advised to share assessments of risk with all professionals involved within area child protection committee umbrellas. The task of undertaking analysis can often profitably involve workers from different agencies (eg a social worker and a probation officer) and decision making on a truly multi-agency basis at case conference can be informed by high quality reports which make transparent the means by which judgements have been made.

Supervision of workers undertaking risk assessment

Work in the area of sexual abuse, to be effective and safe, requires agency ownership that supports clear organisational structures. Morrison (1994) provides a framework of management and organisational building blocks that are a necessary prerequisite for good practice:

1. Recognition of the need to work with sexual abusers
2. Mandate and legitimisation for work with sexual abusers
3. Structures for policy, practice development and leadership
4. Philosophy of intervention
5. Policy and practice guidance
6. Training for managers and practitioners
7. Resources and prioritisation of service delivery
8. Supervision and consultation
9. Staff care policy and provision
10. Evaluation of practice.

This is a formidable list and Morrison & Print (1995) invite readers 'to reflect on the degree to which these elements are present in their own context'. There are clearly significant resource implications in undertaking risk assessments and managers should attempt to be attentive to both structural requirements and the immediate needs of practitioners. For assessors, a critical issue is 'time'. A good assessment cannot be rushed or completed in a couple of sessions. Not only will its conclusions be suspect but professional/client relationships are likely to be left in tatters, which can, in itself have serious consequences for risk management. Briggs et al (1997, p.152) make the point, based on considerable experience, that 'it is very easy to underestimate the amount of time involved in thorough risk assessments. It is best to think in terms of days rather than hours for such an activity'.

Most professionals involved in working with sexually abusive behaviour would advocate that assessments should be co-worked. Whilst this undoubtedly increases staff time committed to the task it is unlikely to double it and the benefits are considerable. Assessment is likely to be more balanced and accurate, the practitioners will feel more confident and safer, issues around difference are more easily monitored and a degree of peer supervision can be encouraged.

Nevertheless, regular supervision is vital and recognised good practice standards should be adhered to (eg see Morrison 1993). In supervising staff in this area of work it is helpful if sessions have included some discussion about the feelings that can be generated about sexual abuse and the theoretical perspectives that are informing the work before supervision around a specific assessment is required. If an assessment is being co-worked, a supervisor will need to give time to addressing issues from the co-working relationship and be prepared to intervene if it is felt that it has become dysfunctional, dangerous, or unsafe.

If consultancy is part of the organisational support being offered, clarity is required about its role and how that relates to those with operational responsibility for the work.

Depending on the other balances and checks in the system, a supervisor may well have a crucial and active role in the undertaking of a risk assessment. This may involve ensuring that:

- the assessor(s) are clear about their role, what they are assessing and why.
- the process is well planned.
- information gathered is ordered in a structured way that enables the supervisor (and ultimately others) to see how conclusions have been drawn.
- assessors keep an 'open mind' during the process through the creative management of professional anxiety. Practitioners need to be supported as they 'worry' about the relative impact of each factor in the situation that they are considering so as to avoid judgements being made which solidify too early in the assessment process and which may skew final conclusions irredeemably.
- confidence and professional integrity are maintained even in the face of strenuous denials, resistance and sometimes hostility and aggression. In particular, assessors may need help in managing feelings of frustration which may result in oppressive practice, the subjects' disengagement and the subsequent loss of important information.
- working with difference does not result in oppressive practice. Assessors should be encouraged to reflect on social and cultural issues which may have a bearing on client participation and the eventual conclusions drawn. Supervision should monitor the relationships within the assessment process to check that the right balance is being struck between encouragement of the clients and the posing of difficult and personally challenging issues.
- Assessors' feelings and 'gut reactions' are acknowledged – again to inform anti-oppressive practice, to maintain the 'open mind approach', and to enable issues of self care to be

addressed. Supervisors can help practitioners to reflect on possible dynamic processes within assessments such as transference, projection etc. Such insights may be important in understanding subjects and facilitating worker self care.

Supervision, as in any social care context, should seek to balance the organisational need for appropriate accountability with the need of individual practitioners to be supported and encouraged. In this area of work particular attention should be given to acknowledging the experiencing of pressure from a number of sources (clients, agencies, systems etc) and feelings of isolation that may result for workers.

Who should undertake assessments?

The choice of workers to undertake assessments of risk is crucial. Practitioners need to be clear with themselves and others about whether they wish to undertake the work. Those who choose not to, for whatever reason, should have that choice respected. A more difficult tension for managers can be dealing with staff who want to undertake the work but whose attitudes and observed behaviour would result in a questioning of their ability to safely do so. The impact of 'personal issues' on ability to undertake risk assessments is potentially very contentious and needs careful handling.

Reservations have already been expressed about workers with insufficient experience being expected to undertake assessments of risk posed by sexually abusive behaviour. To be involved in the assessment process practitioners should, as an absolute minimum, have a good comprehension of the relevant knowledge base, current research etc and have participated in appropriate training. *For workers without these skills, being asked to undertake a risk assessment on their own constitutes poor management practice that should be challenged.*

To be able to lead effectively and take overall responsibility for an assessment, a practitioner should have additionally participated in training that directly addressed issues of risk assessment and management and have experience in working with sexual abusers. As with many challenging tasks, appropriate and well founded confidence in knowledge and skills enables assessors to concentrate on the issues that are raised during the process rather than spending a disproportionate amount of time worrying about their ability to perform adequately in what can be a very stressful situation.

It is often felt that external specialist input is required, and for difficult, complex cases where there is a clear lack of in-house expertise this is entirely appropriate. However, there are significant costs involved in 'buying in' assessments with the implication that they are likely to be restricted by most agencies to the most dangerous or contentious cases. Many local authority social workers will be faced with the need to produce assessments of risk for case conferences, civil courts etc, without the help of specialist input or specialist skills of their own and will often feel under pressure 'to do the best they can'. Practitioners are urged to discuss such dilemmas fully with their line manager in order to reduce the risk of unsafe assessments being produced and to explore options that might improve their adequacy.

If the assessment is to be undertaken on a co-worked basis there is clearly more scope for a relatively less experienced practitioner to be involved alongside a colleague with more specialist skills. Managers need to be creative with the staff resources at their disposal and to forge multi-agency links that may support co-working partnerships. Obvious alliances, for example between probation and local authority social workers, can provide benefits which go beyond the production of an individual assessment in terms of multi-agency working, child protection and skills exchanges.

Establishing and maintaining co-working relationships in order to undertake assessments

Co-working of assessments can provide clear benefits in terms of the accuracy and usefulness of conclusions, and in the support provided to staff. However, establishing and maintaining co-working relationships require a conscious effort - it doesn't just happen! When workers are brought together specifically to undertake a particular assessment (and where it is likely that they represent two separate agencies) much time is required to ensure that they are able to work comfortably with each other as a team.

Erooga (1993) suggests six stages of preparation for co-workers aimed at producing a safe and effective working relationship:

1. *Orientation*
   Workers should explore the context in which they are proposing to work (eg multi-agency perspectives, issues of accountability/responsibility, the impact of differential status etc).

2. *Defining the task*
   Workers should not assume a common understanding of the task. Clarity of aims, objectives and methods is vital.

3. *Contracting*
   Workers are encouraged to make clear agreements about the contents of preparation sessions and of their expectations of their relationship with an external consultant or supervisor.

4. *Sharing information/building trust*
   Ongoing discussions about values, attitudes and theoretical understandings are important in building a solid basis to a co-working relationship. Workers must decide how much personal information they wish to divulge. Exercises that generate lists of 'hopes', 'fears', 'strengths', weaknesses' etc can be particularly useful.

5. *Contracting and problem solving*
   Workers should try to predict the types of difficulties they might encounter while undertaking a piece of work and plan interventions that would address such issues and also be supportive of each other. It is not uncommon in the assessment process for a client to 'target' one of the workers, either because they feel more comfortable with that individual or because they perceive relative vulnerability.

6. *Viability and maintenance*
   Workers (and supervisors) should reflect on whether the co-working team is adequate to the task of assessment and what

is required to maintain healthy functioning over time.

The most efficient (in terms of resources) and effective (in terms of accuracy of assessments) co-working partnerships are those which develop over time and are able to undertake assessments on a regular basis. Many agencies find it difficult to earmark sufficient resources for such specialisation and practitioners may be forced to continually 're-invent the wheel'. However, multi-agency protocols and agreements can be effective in generating pools of workers sharing similar approaches and understandings from which co-working dyads can be drawn as required. Similarly, a degree of specialism in this approach can be particularly beneficial - encouraging such a group to meet on a regular basis can reduce feelings of isolation and maintain a sense of common purpose.

Given the gender dynamics in our society that are viewed as underpinning sexual violence, it is not surprising that most practitioners prefer to work in mixed gender dyads (unless issues specific to the case being considered suggest otherwise). Once again the benefits that accrue from such an approach have to be worked towards and attention given to issues which are specifically gender related.

Richards & Sharkey (1996) make the following points:

- Male workers should analyse and understand their own constructs in relation to male sexuality and patriarchy
- Men should be prepared to give up power
- Gender issues should be a regular slot within debriefing after sessions
- There should be clear boundaries in co-working relationships and a preparedness to talk about intimate issues which impinge upon the professional relationship
- The development of trust requires truth and honesty. An explicit understanding should be reached that if any sexual attraction develops between co-workers it needs to be acknowledged and worked through (with a third party if appropriate)

The importance of taking the time (and courage !) to address these issues is underlined by their cautionary note that otherwise 'assessments of risk may reflect the arguing power of differently gendered workers'.

The professional role

Workers undertaking assessments should be clear about their role within the process and the need to maintain it over time. Ownership of personal issues relating to sex, sexual abuse, relationships etc has already been highlighted and should be viewed as a necessary prerequisite in separating the personal from the professional whilst engaging in the process. In particular, assessors should be clear that they are not prepared to discuss their own personal 'stuff' in assessment sessions even though the expectations on subjects to do just that are considerable. Assessment of complicated behaviour and situations is simply not possible if workers are struggling to deal with issues relating to them personally.

Assessment requires that those involved retain an 'open minded' approach that social workers undertaking child protection investigations will readily recognise. As mentioned above, this, if correctly maintained will generate considerable anxiety which requires acknowledgement and management. It is crucial that such concerns are not denied but rather worked with as an essential check in the process of synthesising information and producing judgements.

The Children Act 1989 makes it clear that the needs of the child are paramount and careful thought should be given to how to maintain a focus on the best interests of the child without becoming an advocate for the child in the assessment. Markham (1997) points out that 'workers who 'take the child into the assessment with them' run the risk of significantly distorting the dynamics of the process and fueling resistance from the subjects'.

Resistance is almost certainly going to be evident where abuse is strenuously denied by a client. It is easy for workers to be drawn into a lengthy debate about whether abusive incidents have taken place or not, which can result in unproductive 'stand offs' caricatured by exchanges such as 'I didn't do it' .... 'Yes you did!' Workers within the criminal justice field can distance themselves from such tensions by referring to the authority of the court, but where there is no conviction the legitimacy of the assessment is likely to be highly contentious. Alleged abusers will easily argue that they can pose no risk as they weren't abusive in the first place, although a finding of fact from a civil court may help clarify the situation. The less that an alleged abuser acknowledges abusive behaviour the more crucial it is that assessors attend to the nature of their role and are able to demonstrate an even-handed approach throughout the process of evidence accumulation.

Planning risk assessments

Clarity is essential in planning a risk assessment. It is often important to make the distinction between a 'therapeutic input' and an 'assessment'. When assessing, the primary focus must be on understanding and prediction of risk, (its potential for management, change etc) rather than on stimulating change in itself. Of course, there may well be some change in attitudes, behaviours, degree of responsibility taken etc as a direct result of the assessment process itself. This may provide important information about the potential for the subjects to engage in ongoing work, cooperate with monitoring strategies and, indeed change. However, assessors should be wary of being drawn into repeated attempts to 'move the client forward' as the task of assessment is essentially one of engagement, observation and interpretation. Resistance should be noted, as should any response to challenge, and the assessor is often best advised to then move on to other areas.

Even when time is particularly short, the benefits of planning an assessment cannot be over-emphasised. An overall plan of proposed sessions indicating which areas of work are to be covered and allowing sufficient time for analysis of the information gained and presentation of conclusions to be written up is essential if maximum use of the time available is to be made. Once again clarity is required to determine:

• the expectations of the assessment (initial/comprehensive).
• what information is required and from which sources.

- who is to be directly interviewed.
- where and when assessment sessions will take place.

In family situations consideration must be given to the extent of involvement in the process of a non-abusing partner. In general, the more involvement the better, as involvement provides a partner, and potential protector of the children, with the opportunity to listen to the details of previous abusive behaviour, its likely impact on victims, professionals views on risk and the requirements for its safe management. This process can be particularly empowering of women who may have heard only a sanitised version of previous abuse from their male partners and may also witness rationalisations and minimisations challenged for the first time. There is, therefore, the potential for such inclusion to provide an educative component that may directly enhance a non-abusing partner's ability to protect children in the future. Of course, a partner's response to the content of the sessions, including professionals' challenges and interpretations, will also provide valuable evidence of her attitude to risk, the need for risk management and the likelihood of adequate protection being provided to the children.

It has to be recognised, however, that inclusion of a non-abusing partner in the whole process may prove too threatening to some abusers and result in increased resistance and denial. In such situations it may be more productive to negotiate for a partner to be involved in the initial stages (where the purpose and plan is outlined) and then to rejoin the process for consideration of the conclusions reached.

Where children are potentially at risk, their views on any proposed rehabilitation are obviously vital, as is an assessment of their ability to (appropriately) protect themselves. Whilst this will require some direct interviewing, care should be taken not to subject children to repeats of previous information gathering exercises, particularly about abusive incidents. Before direct engagement with children to explore issues of risk etc all existing sources of information should be collated and reviewed (eg video interviews, case conference minutes etc).

Prior to meeting with any of the subjects it is advisable to collate and review information that is available from other sources (agency records, criminal records, statements to police etc) and to allow sufficient time for their impact to have been absorbed. Workers who read highly distressing victim statements, for example, immediately before interviewing an abuser may well find their emotional response difficult to manage. In such situations it is not uncommon for an abuser to detect very strong negative feelings at a time when the process requires that he is reassured and invited to be as honest as possible.

When planning an assessment process it is not advisable to follow a set format as the needs of each case will be unique, requiring careful thought about what type of process is likely to provide the best results. Nevertheless, there are some common themes and tasks in all assessment processes. The City Team, South Yorkshire Probation Service (Gocke & Markham, 1997), developed the following structure around which individual assessments were tailored:

1. *Introductions*
   - Statements about the purpose of the sessions and theoretical base
   - Proposed methods to be used
   - Contracting (how assessor/subject relationships will be managed)
   - Setting of homework
   - 'abuser's story about the abuse'

2. *Consideration of abuse details*
   - Discussion and clarification
   - Comparison with other sources of information (eg police depositions)
   - Setting of homework
   - 'consequences for victim(s)'

3. *Exploration of victim empathy*
   - Abuser's ability to put self in a victim's shoes and understand the immediate and longer term consequences of abuse. (As noted in chapter 3, assessors should be particularly careful not to try and address rationalisations and minimisations in this area but be content to note them at this stage.)

4. *Analysis of known abusive behaviour*
   • Multi-factor analysis (flip charted 'live')

5. *Analysis of current and likely future situation*
   • Multi-factor analysis (flip charted 'live')

6. *Consideration of risk and its potential for management*
   • Significant risk factors (including 'static' factors and their significance)
   • Triggers
   • Likely risky situations
   • Controls and monitoring

7. *Conclusions and proposals*
   • Synthesis of information gathered
   • Subjects' views of the assessment
   • Detailed proposals for management if appropriate
   • Planned future work

The team found that the length of time devoted to each area could vary significantly and that it was therefore difficult to estimate the number of sessions required for an assessment. To some extent the amount of time available (to meet external deadlines) largely dictated how this was planned, with an acknowledgement that this could have a significant impact on quality. It was possible to undertake an assessment allocating one $1^1/_2$ hr session for each of the above areas over a period of 3-4 weeks, although the amount of time available to 'draw an abuser into the process' in these situations was severely limited. Assessments that allowed more sessions with increased flexibility over longer periods often increased participation by the subjects, with the result that plans made for management of risk were usually more fully 'owned' and likely to be more robust.

In addition to planning the overall shape of an assessment, consideration is also necessary to ensure that each individual session is well thought out and reviewed at its conclusion. Time should be put aside before the subjects arrive to ensure that the assessors are clear about the issues they wish to address and the techniques they intend using. Immediately following an interview is a good time to discuss the key points that have arisen and to plan the next session. De-briefing can be a continuation of this process. Approximately 1hr 45m needs to be set aside for a 1hr interview to allow enough time for all the tasks, including 15 minutes for preparation and 30 minutes for review and debriefing. Of course some sessions can be particularly complicated and harrowing and workers will feel the need for more time to be set aside following their completion.

Engaging subjects in the assessment process

Assessments of sexually abusive behaviour are by necessity largely worker dominated. Assessors clarify the purpose of the task, the methods that will be used and the means by which conclusions will be drawn. In very crude terms the dynamics of such a situation can be characterised thus. The abuser (and other family members) have the power of information (about previous abuse, current risks, motivations etc). The professionals have the mandated power of statutory intervention underpinned by a commonly agreed clinical knowledge base. The task of the professional is to elicit sufficient information to make a useful assessment. For many abusers the perceived aim is to provide only such information as is likely to produce a positive assessment from their point of view.

Reference to the sexual assault cycle reviewed in Chapter 2 suggests that abusers can become highly competent in manipulating people and situations when planning and abusing. Those skills are unfortunately transferable to the assessment process, and workers will become aware of attempts by many abusers to manipulate them regarding what is discussed and how information is interpreted. Most unnerving for professionals is the realisation that successful manipulation implies their being unaware that it has taken place!

Other attempts at manipulation maybe more obvious, but nevertheless still difficult to deal with. Anger and verbal aggression on the part of subjects can effectively block the progress of an assessment and often leave assessors 'rattled' and unsure how to proceed. Despite such difficulties, it is important that workers act with confidence and appropriate authority, if the process is to continue and the assessment is to be usefully completed.

Workers will be very aware of the tensions that such dynamics frequently produce and the consequent difficulties in completing assessments which are 'fair' to the adults involved while maintaining the necessary focus on the needs and future safety of children. Managing these dynamics is often the crucial task in the undertaking of assessments where a specific family situation is being considered and where there is little concrete information available. This requires considerable skill and creativity.

The insights from 'motivational interviewing' (Miller & Rollnick, 1991), while primarily developed in relation to longer term work, are also important when considering how to engage with the people who are to be assessed. Workers must be aware of the ambivalences likely to be felt by an abuser who is faced with a discussion of personally challenging issues and with invitations to take responsibility for abusive behaviour. For many abusers a part of them is likely to want to discuss their behaviour and attempt to make some sense of it for themselves. Another, often more prevalent part will (particularly in an assessment), be motivated to avoid this at all costs, generating a defensive and potentially resistant attitude towards the process. Working with ambivalence is often a key component of the overall task and appropriate acknowledgement should be made of any progress made and of evidence of increased honesty or motivation to tackle difficult matters.

As suggested in chapter 3, particular care is required in deciding how challenges are made to statements by an abuser which appear to deny/minimise/rationalise key elements of the situation. 'Pushing someone into a corner' by reacting strongly and negatively to comments made should be avoided wherever possible. Abusers appear to have particular difficulty in acknowledging the following:

- 'NOT OK' sexual arousal (due to the intimate nature of the information and the fear of being branded as 'deviant').
- the planning of the abuse (because to do so accepts premeditation, which is often viewed as casting the resultant behaviour in a worse light).
- that they pose a risk for the future (as they wish to impress upon the assessors that they are safe, and are probably highly motivated to convince themselves of this!)

When such resistance begins to occur workers would do well to remind themselves that they are assessing behaviours, attitudes and responses to intervention rather than (at that point) trying to change them! Assessments should aim to identify cognitive distortions and evaluate the potential that subjects may have to question them.

A careful balance needs to be struck as some direct challenging will have to occur if an abuser's potential response to future intervention is to be evaluated and assessors must be careful not to be seen to collude with cognitive distortions that become manifest. The following techniques may be useful:

- choose when not to comment on a statement that is contentious (and be careful not to automatically nod the head).
- register difficulties in accepting a view but suggest returning to the issue at a later date.
- exhibit 'puzzlement' rather than disagreement (which can be especially useful when contradictions begin to appear in accounts of what happened and why).
- seek clarification and/or express an inability to understand.

As a rule of thumb direct challenges should not be made until the assessment process is well established. This should ensure that any tensions thus generated are in the context of a professional relationship that has at least begun to develop and therefore more likely to be successfully worked through. Another, entirely pragmatic reason for following this advice, is that it reduces the likelihood of subjects withdrawing early in the process - with a consequent loss of vital information.

As in most human interactions, first impressions can be very important in setting the tone of subsequent relationships. The first meeting with the subjects is crucial in establishing a working relationship that has the potential to provide sufficient good quality information that will aid accurate assessment. The following issues may usefully be addressed:

- Review the reasons for the assessment to ensure there are no basic misunderstandings.

- Provide information about the structure and process of assessment (but being careful not to give rigid time boundaries for the component tasks).
- Make clear the limits of confidentiality with regard to information disclosed and the duty of the assessors to inform the relevant statutory agencies should they become aware of any child currently at risk or of abusive incidents that have not already been investigated.
- Explain the role of the assessor, giving a commitment to maintaining an open mind whilst the information is being gathered and made sense of.
- Acknowledge the difficulties involved in talking about the subject matter and the high stakes involved.
- Discuss the difficulties and tensions that are likely to be generated within the process and seek agreement on how these might be managed.
- Reassure subjects that their views will be included within the completed assessment even if they are at odds with the conclusions reached.

Assessors should be encouraged to use the discussion of the above points to draw up a 'contract' that informs how the assessment will proceed and how the various parties are expected to behave within it. This can provide a vital reference point at a later time when difficulties may begin to feel unmanageable and threaten the viability of the whole assessment. Contracting also formalises and makes explicit the dynamics between subjects and assessors and invites the former to take a share of the responsibility to make the process work.

Opinions differ on when is the most productive moment for assessors to provide subjects with an overview of the knowledge base that will be used in the interpretation of information gathered. Fisher & Howard (1993) advocate a clear set of statements at the beginning of the process whilst The City Team found that such information was better left until the stage of the assessment where interpretations are being made. Providing such details at the outset can often result in confrontation and misunderstandings right at the point where all efforts should be focused on setting up good working relationships. Subjects, who are understandably apprehensive and keen to 'make the right impression', may well then try to modify their responses to questions on the basis of their understanding of the professionals' perspective. Again assessors are encouraged to weigh up the particular circumstances of the case – it would clearly be farcical not to allude to the knowledge base at the outset when assessing a convicted abuser who had considerable experience of previous assessments and intervention programmes!

Subjects should be involved in the interpretation of the information gathered and the conclusions that are drawn. This can have an educational impact, clarifying the professionals' view of the nature and extent of the risks and expectations regarding future management, which can be particularly empowering of non-abusing partners. It is, of course, also an opportunity for subjects to offer alternative interpretations of the evidence gathered which should be included in any final report as agreed in the initial contracting. It is often at this point that tensions which have been 'simmering', but managed within the process, begin to surface. It is only fair that subjects are given some time to assimilate the judgements that are being made before their response is included in the final report (which is another argument for clear initial planning which avoids assessments being hurriedly drawn together at the last moment). If it is felt that there is potential for the risks identified to be managed within a family situation then it is obviously important that the adults involved continue to be included within the process and motivated to continue their cooperation.

Methods

Practitioners use and adapt different exercises from books, training courses and other workers. This discussion explores the most commonly used method of assessment - that of the 'structured interview' involving questions, answers, and hopefully discussion.

The knowledge base suggests that abusers are likely to be both motivated and adept at diversionary, deflectionary tactics. Workers, therefore, must interview in detail as discussion about generalisations will inevitably result in superficial and potentially unsafe judgements. Interviewing in detail about sexually abusive behaviour can in itself be stressful and difficult to manage, but precise information about abusive incidents, planning, fantasy etc is required. Workers must be able, when appropriate, to lead discussion that refers to intimate body parts and the distressing human dynamics of victimisation.

For the most part this results in workers taking on a directive style, ensuring that key issues are addressed despite difficult feelings being generated. This too requires care and a balanced approach, generating sufficient gravity to reflect the seriousness of the issues under consideration whilst not 'tipping over' into bullying, condemning and of course, ultimately, 'nonce bashing' (Sheath, 1990). Being openly dismissive of explanations that are offered by subjects will almost certainly generate resistance and may result in states of anger and/or high anxiety. This should ring warning bells for workers who have evidence (or suspect) that these factors have figured in the build up to previous abuse. The potential for such exchanges within the assessment contributing to current, and, sometimes immediate, risk should not be forgotten, and interviews managed accordingly.

Directive questioning should also be balanced with open ended questions and invitations to the subjects to develop discussion around issues they feel are important or of concern to them. Adequate assessments require information about what subjects think, not what they think assessors want them to say and thus care must be taken not to ask leading questions or over-pressurise for a response. The appropriate use (and timing) of silence can be a skill of considerable importance when discussing emotive issues.

Time should be built in to the end of every assessment session for subjects to 'come down' from the issues being discussed. In many situations a direct question of 'how are you feeling' permits acknowledgement of the difficulties being experienced and for the conversation to then move onto more mundane matters such as confirmation of next session, updates about criminal justice or civil law processes.

However the interviews are conducted, the information gleaned must be recorded, a role often assigned to co-workers! This will probably involve frantic scribbling with the occasional interjection to clarify something, whilst the other worker leads and shapes the discussion. Roles can be swapped around, from session to session or within sessions.

A more dynamic way of recording information which is potentially more inclusive of the subjects is to flip chart 'live' key issues, opinions, etc. Ideally, the abuser should do the writing (encouraging ownership and responsibility taking) but this requires considerable literacy and cognitive skills – which may deflect attention and concentration from the key task of engaging with the issues. A good compromise is for a worker to do the writing but to try and capture the essence of the discussions and points made. Use of first person quotes is recommended.

Flip charting in this way can allow 'the story of the abuse' to be initially drafted by the abuser and then amended during discussion in the session. On many occasions a decision will be made to flip chart the initial draft of 'the story' live in the session. Similarly, building up an understanding of the factors involved can be done on flip charts (one for each heading of the multi-factor structure), making the mechanics of assessment more transparent and understandable to subjects and likely to be better owned by them when risk management strategies are being considering. This approach combines the task of recording with an effective method of evidence accumulation, even though practitioners can become surrounded by walls of flip charts! It encourages the identification of links and contradictions and enables a second worker to play a much more active part in the process. Indeed, many workers will both lead a session and flip chart, leaving the second worker to occupy a more reflective position that allows for significant interventions.

Other uses of flip charts may include:

- Cartooning - a pictorial account of an abusive incident.
- Drawing of maps, plans of houses, rooms etc.
- Pie charts - to elicit proportions of 'OK'/'NOT OK' fantasies.
- Force field analysis - to depict the relative risks and potential controls.
- Life histories, 'life lines', 'life graphs'.

There is considerable scope for such exercises to be set as homework, enabling more efficient use of the time within sessions, placing a clear responsibility on an abuser to engage in the process and providing a measure for assessment of motivation. However, as noted above, this requires considerable skills which many subjects will not have. Indeed the whole process of structured interviews assumes a whole array of cognitive and social skills on the part of those involved. In particular, the above method is over reliant on reasonable literacy skills, although drawings and making of audio tapes may be used to supplement/complement this.

Inclusiveness of subjects in the assessment exercise is clearly a major goal that requires creativity, and commitment to try out different exercises, media and strategies. It is also reliant on workers having a clear grasp of the stratifications within our society and the impact that power relationships can have on interactions within the assessment process and the judgements subsequently made.

Working with difference

As in all areas of intervention into people's lives, it is crucial that workers are committed to an anti-oppressive approach to practice that recognises issues around difference. Risk assessments are often undertaken in a context of emotional tension where the stakes for the subjects are very high. The nature of the content matter – sexually abusive behaviour – means that the process itself can easily become oppressive. Assessors should be careful with the terminology they employ and take time to contextualise issues (eg 'most people masturbate and fantasise ....', 'most people would find talking about this difficult .....'). Workers need to be particularly aware of their potential to be oppressive and must seek to provide a quality service to people from all groups in our society - and particularly children!

It is particularly worth noting that a key element in any analysis of the potential to manage risk effectively will be the perception of the likely cooperation of the subject(s) with statutory agencies. Clearly this is a dynamic that may well be significantly distorted by prejudice (conscious or subconscious) on the part of workers and an understandable lack of trust felt by subjects whose experience of oppression in society at large may be considerable. Once again the concept of 'a balanced approach' is useful. Workers should take care to minimise the negative impact of discrimination whilst ensuring that important issues are not 'ducked' for fear of allegations being made of being oppressive. This section briefly considers some of the key factors that may generate oppressive practice and result in unsafe assessments.

Race

Shergill & Afzal Khan (1997) identify four key factors to be considered when working with black people who have committed sexually abusive behaviour:

1. *Motivation*
   For black people, having to engage with agencies of social control which are essentially white is likely to create barriers. Previous experiences of racism make it difficult for black abusers to have confidence, when working through difficult and personally threatening issues, that they will be treated with respect and dealt with competently by white workers.

2. *Denial and minimisation*
   Resistance to the taking of responsibility by black abusers may in part be the product of a habituated response to previously experienced racism. However, workers must test out with care any assertions that allegations of abuse are essentially racist, and avoid collusion with cognitive distortions that seek to maintain denial.

   Black abusers and their families may on occasion experience strong pressures to deny and minimise from within their own cultures and communities (to a significant extent the result of habituated defensiveness in the face of persistent racism). As with all families and communities, collusion on the part of significant others may be a significant factor in assessment.

3. *Assumptions and stereotypes carried by workers*
   White workers must be careful to acknowledge to themselves the presence of ideological racist stereotypes that may distort their approach to assessment. These include: the myth of the black rapist; the notion that black women are promiscuous; and the black abuser/white victim caricature.

4. *Internalised racism*

    For any abuser, seriously addressing their sexually abusive behaviour requires considerable commitment and courage. Black abusers will struggle even more so if they find themselves in a position where they feel they have to deny their own identity. Moreover, internalised racism may generate increased defensiveness and resistance to considering ambivalences held about abusive behaviour.

Most workers would acknowledge the need for appropriate consultancy and interpretation services to be available to aid the process of assessment in such circumstances. However, it is also important that white workers feel empowered to take on the role of assessors when working cross-culturally, and avoid the routine 'dumping' of such cases onto black workers.

Gender

Much has already been made of the centrality of gendered power relations in the context and commissioning of sexually abusive behaviour. These dynamics will continue to be a significant presence within assessment. Although the inclusion of non-abusing partners (usually female) has been depicted above as providing the potential to empower women, care must still be taken not to inadvertently compound gender stereotypes. The nature of the interactions between male/female workers and male/female subjects should be monitored with care. Avoid giving the impression that a male worker always takes the lead while the female worker appears to undertake the more supportive tasks of note taking etc; efforts should be made to draw a 'quiet' female subject into the discussions and not allow a dominant male to answer questions on her behalf. Of course, workers should also be aware of the potential consequences for women who may be in violent relationships if discussions within the sessions directly address issues of power imbalances within the family situation.

How a male subject reacts to male/female workers can also be very instructive. It is not unusual for a male abuser to try to develop a relationship with the male worker to the exclusion of the female worker, or to seek a more sympathetic response from the female. Female co-workers are often acutely aware of distorted dynamics based on gender and their experiences should be explored within the process of assessment and used to inform judgements made.

This book, for reasons that have been explained, has concentrated almost entirely on considering issues around male sexual abusers. However, the assessments occasionally required of female abusers typically create considerable difficulties for workers, as such situations challenge most of our implicit assumptions about who is responsible for sexual abuse. Assessors need to remind themselves that this may result in victims not being believed or their experiences minimised (especially if you are dealing with an adolescent boy abused by a woman; this may be seen as a form of 'initiation' rather than the sexual abuse which it is). Many practitioners, when considering their evaluation, often seek to ensure a balanced approach by posing the question 'how might our analysis be different if the abuser was male ?'

Sexual orientation

Sexual orientation can be a difficult subject for many people, workers and clients alike. There are many issues to consider, not least of all whether the person is 'in' or 'out'. For many, being open about their sexuality, in a society that discriminates against sexual preferences that are different, is very difficult. We may be asking perpetrators to talk about homosexual or bisexual preferences for the first time as well as requiring them to talk about sexually abusive behaviour.

The generalised homophobic discrimination in our society contains a specific myth that gay men represent an indiscriminate and high risk to young boys. For gay men who are abusers this may result in double discrimination and an understandable reluctance to discuss their sexual behaviour and preferences within assessment. It may be appropriate to address such issues directly in an attempt to reassure subjects that their fears are understood and that every effort will be made to ensure a fair assessment. This may be easier said than done and workers should examine themselves very closely to see whether these issues constitute prejudicial blocks to good practice for them.

For women who are lesbian this can pose even more complex problems. For example a women may not trust her co-workers enough to inform them of her sexuality. This may mean at the very basic level having to work in a 'heterosexist' environment that assumes heterosexuality is 'normal' and anything else is not. There may be jokes as well as assumptions which will make the workers position very uncomfortable. For women perpetrators, as with male perpetrators who are homosexual, there is the often-made link in society (reflected by some workers) that the very nature of homosexuality encompasses a sexual attraction to children. Homosexual men can be seen in this light, as can lesbian women who emphasise gender characteristics commonly attributed to men.

Some workers reading this may feel that it does not apply to them. Sadly this is far from true and any concerned worker who takes the time to talk to gay and lesbian friends will find that, for all, there is the constant battle against assumption and oppression. This is often exacerbated by the unconscious behaviour of some male co-workers who may appear to give up some power to 'straight' women, but behave very differently towards lesbian women or gay men. Sexuality and gender is often not looked at honestly in co-working or colleague relationships, and this omission can do irreparable damage to workers self-esteem and the task in hand, that of producing risk assessments that are objective, transparent and equitable.

Learning disability

Before any risk assessment is undertaken of an abuser with learning disabilities, it is essential that an assessment of cognitive functioning is referred to, or commissioned. This will inform both the evaluation made, and the methods employed in the process.

Learning disability raises complicated issues about the attribution of responsibility for abusive acts and the degree to which meaningful cooperation with risk management strategies can be expected. Workers must take great care to ensure that abusers understand what is being asked of them and of the concepts being employed. This typically involves considerable patience, the use of creative methods and an acceptance that the process may well take considerably longer because of this. Consultancy from specialist practitioners may be particularly useful in these situations.

Care must be taken to ensure the abuser's civil rights are not abnegated, particularly if the risk assessment is being undertaken prior to sentencing. It may be useful to have an independent advocate present.

Physical disability

Workers need to be respectful and understanding of an abuser's physical disabilities and ensure that issues around access to buildings, offices etc are thought through in advance of assessments commencing. On many occasions physical disabilities will be used by abusers to ridicule allegations that may have been made and to argue that it is impossible for them to pose a serious risk in the future. Such assertions must be dealt with sensitively—workers should seek evidence on the precise impact of the disabilities from other sources, and avoiding being drawn by invitations to pity the individual and thus absolve them from full responsibility.

Age

A central theme in considering child sexual abuse is that of the power dynamics inherent in interactions between adults and children. Workers need to retain a 'child focused' approach even although the majority of assessment time will involve engaging with the adults in the situation. This is not easy, particularly given the discrimination against children in our society and the concentration on the rights and civil liberties of adults often at the expense of the consideration of their responsibilities to children.

The criminal law's central tenet of 'innocent until proved guilty' provides a powerful justification for concerns to shield adults from false accusations made by children. Clearly children can lie about abusive incidents but the research would suggest that, contrary to popular opinion, children do not routinely lie about important issues, although they may be particularly sensitive to the reactions of adults that they are telling. In situations where children's credibility is being questioned because of their age, workers need to maintain a balanced approach that is not collusive.

Elderly abusers pose a different set of challenges, with workers needing to be sensitive to the difficulties that old age can generate in respect of access, hearing etc. Again care is required not to collude with cognitive distortions that are based on age, particularly suggestions that future risk can be dismissed as a physical impossibility. The difficulty is compounded if the abuser is suffering from a degenerative condition such as Alzheimer's, associated with impaired memory and attention.

Using behaviour within the process as material for assessment

Most information gathered during assessment is mediated by other people, professionals, subjects etc. However, the process itself can provide opportunities to directly observe behaviours and interactions, which may also inform the assessment, particularly with regard to the potential for risk management.

How adult partners interact within interviews can provide insight into the dynamics of the home situation, and the likelihood of the non-abusing partner being able to provide adequate protection to the children. Similarly, how subjects respond to challenge will indicate their likely ability to work within the controls and restraints of a child protection plan.

Nevertheless, caution is necessary, and too much store should not be placed on information from one source on its own. The behaviour manifested in assessments must to a considerable extent be a product of that very unusual and pressurised situation. Subjects who frequently lose their temper or become aggressive may well be responding to the uncertainties of the situation and may yet cooperate adequately with subsequent monitoring once the assessment is known and complete. Other subjects who appear to be motivated within the series of interviews may be working hard to create a favourable impression and later may not cooperate with risk management strategies as expected.

Report writing

A well-conducted risk assessment will generate a large amount of information which should be organised and rationalised during the process of analysis and evaluation. Even if this has been done efficiently, the task of presenting the conclusions in a report can be daunting. Assessors should be mindful of the arena in which the report will be required (case conference, court etc), and of the amount of information that can be reasonably taken in by the professionals and parents involved in the time available. If a commitment to multi-agency working is to be upheld, other professionals should be able to comprehend how and why conclusions have been drawn and to understand in detail any proposals for the management of risk. The combination of a report which summarises key factors considered in assessment, the conclusions drawn and recommendations made, with a series of appendices which give access to the detail of the assessment, can provide a manageable format through which to present and record an assessment.

Assessors should be encouraged to decide what type of report format would best suit the assessment and the needs of all involved. Practitioners tend to develop their own styles and structures but the following outline may be of use:

1. *The basis of the report*
    The mandate and competence of the assessors.

2. *The relevant knowledge base*
    Assessors should make clear the theoretical and research basis for the judgements made. It may be helpful to provide some detail about a particular aspect of the knowledge base if it informs about a significant factor highlighted by the assessment (eg 'denial' - where an abuser is denying future risk).

3. *The process of assessment*
    A short overview of how the assessment has been conducted (interviews, researching records, methods used etc. can provide a useful context and indicate the amount of work that has been undertaken (which in itself should be an indicator of the likely comprehensiveness of the assessment.

4. *The nature of the concerns/allegations*
   The reasons for the assessment should be clearly stated and an overview of the concerns that it addresses. Static variables such as convictions, allegations, investigations should be included here.

5. *Analysis of the nature and extent of the risk posed*
   This section might comprise the key factors identified through the use of the second section of the multi-factor format, with the interpretations that have been made clearly detailed.

6. *Analysis of the potential for risk management*
   Based on the third section of the multi-factor format, this can comprise a review of the proposed circumstances of the family, the identification of risky situations and the possibilities for managing risk safely therein.

7. *Conclusions and recommendations*
   This section should draw the assessment together, making judgements where possible and detailing significant omissions. The implications for the future management of risk should be clearly outlined and reference made to any detailed plan.

8. *Subject's response to the assessment*
   This provides a space for the subject's views and response to the assessment which should indicate the extent to which the document can form the basis of an agreement with parents to work in partnership and implement an agreed plan or strategy.

9. *Appendices*
   - Detailed risk management plan (including arrangements for review).
   - Overview of known abusive behaviour
   - Multi-factor format – key points

Such reports involve a considerable amount of effort, but can often save time in the longer term – especially when regular reviews are required to monitor the situation and to assess risk over time. To obtain maximum benefit it is essential that reports are circulated prior to core groups, case conferences, multi-agency planning meetings etc so that professionals can make properly informed decisions on the basis of their contents. Sufficient time to enable this happen must be built into the planning of the process so that the often experienced last-minute report writing does not occur!

Risk assessments and multi-agency working

Ensuring that situations where children are in need of protection are adequately managed, requires a genuinely multi-agency approach. Nevertheless, relations between agencies can sometimes make this difficult and in themselves undermine risk management strategies. Dangerous working relationships may include:

- Undefined boundaries to roles and responsibilities
- An absence of clear, written procedures to guide intervention
- The existence of hidden agendas that affect formal activity
- The presence of competition and hostility between professionals
- The avoidance of overt disagreement about the management of cases

Inclusion of all involved professionals in decision making on the basis of a formal assessment of risk should clarify the issues at stake and promote multi-agency ownership of plans for monitoring and control.

Assessment of risk with absolute denial

Many workers are faced with situations where there is almost complete denial of the concerns raised and a consequent resistance to the assessment. As already stated, absolute denial must not, in itself be directly equated with 'high risk', although a subject's ability to cooperate with risk management strategies are likely to be questioned.

All assessments are dependent on information being made available to enable analysis to take place. Even when working with an abuser who is acknowledging that abuse has taken place and that future risk must be actively managed, assessment is fraught with difficulty, hindered as it will almost certainly be by cognitive distortions and manipulations.

If perpetration of abuse in the past is acknowledged but current and future risk denied (which is very typically the case) then it is likely that sufficient information will be given to enable an assessment of the nature of the risk posed to be made. Such an exercise may well then prove effective in motivating the subject(s) to reconsider their perception of current and future risk.

Assessments are particularly difficult where the allegations of abuse (and so, necessarily, of risk) are denied. Practitioners are often left with what they would consider to be essential gaps in information and consequently may feel that attempts at assessment are meaningless. Whilst acknowledging this dilemma, there are many such situations where decisions about children's welfare have to be made (at conference, court etc) and professional assessments are required to inform such deliberations.

Gocke & Markham (1997) suggest that multi-factor formats can still be of use in such situations, providing as they do a structure around which an assessment can take place.

1. Basic information

There may be very little information offered that relates directly to the allegations of sexual abuse. However, other recorded offences may be relevant (eg those of violence) as may be evidence of general rule breaking.

More information should be available regarding the alleged abuser's background and personal development. Clearly resistance to provide details in this area would be a cause for particular concern.

2. Analysis of abusive behaviour

Absolute denial of abuse will have severe consequences for the usefulness of this section. Information will available from the allegations but its quality will be dependent on the age of the child, whether there is a video interview, corroborating medical evidence etc.

Nevertheless attempts should be made to elicit self report from the alleged abuser and to obtain some understanding of the subject's explanation for the allegation.

Abuser's sexual motivation to abuse

It is necessary to discuss why this section is so important and to invite comment from the subject. However, unless a sudden 'conversion' occurs, it would be naive to expect much information about this from someone who is denying abuse. Over enthusiastic pursuit of details may precipitate angry withdrawal by an abuser from the process with a subsequent loss of further, important information.

Overcoming internal inhibitors

Some discussion about the significance of this concept can be carefully undertaken, particularly as the final report will undoubtedly discuss implications of denial in general.

Information about external factors may be more readily available eg stress, substance abuse etc.

Insights into the subject's attitudes towards children will be useful.

Circumventing external inhibitors

Information may be available from the details of the allegations made and deductions made about how a child might have been isolated. Retrospective perceptions of non-abusing partners may also be useful. Details about the nature of the relationship between partners can be gleaned from interviews and observations.

Overcoming victim resistance

Details of the process of abuse will again be largely dependent on the allegations made, but contextual information may be more readily available about adult/child relationships within the family.

3. Analysis of current circumstances

Even where abuse (and/or risk) is denied, assessing the circumstances in which risk must be managed should elicit a considerable amount of relevant information.

Abuser's current sexual motivations

It is unlikely that much information will be forthcoming from someone who is protesting their innocence. Clearly, subjects engaging more fully in the process may attempt to manipulate the assessment of future risk. However, recording the subject's views on this area remains an important exercise in demonstrating an open mind.

Abuser's maintenance of internal controls

Assessing current cognitive distortions will be difficult except in a general sense. There may be external factors that remain relevant (eg mental health problems, stressors etc). It would be important to record how an alleged abuser now views the child who made the allegation.

Effectiveness of external controls

Potentially risk situations can be hypothesised and responses of the subject(s) noted. Of particular interest will be the attitude of a non-abusing partner and this might have changed during the process of assessment. One of the key aims of such assessments must be to increase non-abusing partners' knowledge of the allegations and potential risk.

Potential victims

Children potentially at risk are normally readily identifiable and assessment may be made of the appropriateness of self protection work, their views on the allegations, rehabilitation etc.

4. Conclusions

Where considerable denial is experienced and/or significant resistance to the assessment, the judgements made will obviously have to be circumscribed by the lack of key pieces of information.

In some circumstances professionals will be expected to comment on the likelihood of the abuse having taken place and will need couch their assertions in terms of on the 'balance of probabilities'.

Where concerns about the safety of children remain very high in the face of a continuing refusal to cooperate by parents, social workers will have to consider initiating care proceedings and inviting a civil court to judge the competence of their assessments.

Risk assessment: A task worth doing

For workers, the process of assessing the risk to children posed by an abuser or alleged abuser can be daunting and the stress of making professional judgements considerable. Nevertheless, risk assessments are an essential component of child protection plans, and it is to be hoped that professionals will seek out the necessary training to enable them to participate in such a vital task. Workers who can reference the knowledge base and have an understanding of assessment should be able to participate more fully in multi-agency discussion, decision-making and actioning. Child protection plans could be more precise and effective, enabling rigorous management of risk and better safeguards for individual children.

Chapter 8

Change, monitoring and containment:

A selective overview of the nature and efficacy of professional interventions with child sexual abusers

Dan Grant

Refrain I must, What is the cause?
Sure, as they say, 'So Hawks be taught'
But in my case layeth no such clause
For with such craft I am not caught.
('Such hap as I am happed in') Sir Thomas Wyatt (1503-42)

With affection beaming in one eye,
and calculation out of the other.
(Mrs Todgers) Charles Dickens (1812-70)

Introduction

In this chapter we deal very practically with currently popular methods of professional intervention with child sexual abusers. For the reader with little or no experience of this work we provide many references to further reading, while, for those with more experience, attention is drawn throughout this chapter to the recurrent themes of effective practice and research.

The three broad areas to which we turn in this chapter are change, monitoring and containment. Let us first look briefly at the topics we will cover:

- First, we examine some of the current thinking about change, and discuss treatment methods aimed at convincing abusers, often by therapeutic or educative means, to change or control their behaviour.
- Second, the issue of containment is explored, which, as we shall see, deals with risk management.
- Third, we concentrate on child sexual abusers who escape prosecution and who are not subject to a finding of fact in civil proceedings.
- Fourth, we review relevant effectiveness research.
- Finally, we investigate relapse prevention techniques.

Your attention will have already been drawn, elsewhere in this book, to the substantial under reporting of sexual crime, and subsequently, the even lower (some may say unbelievably low) rates of prosecution and conviction. It follows, that most child sexual abusers brought to the attention of professionals working in child protection will not have been convicted. This is clearly an unsatisfactory and disappointing position, not least because a lack of statutory recognition by the criminal justice system often impedes attempts to engage perpetrators in methods of control. Accordingly, our concern here is to examine what can be done to intervene effectively to protect children, and to see how we might assist perpetrators to change, or control, their behaviour. To illustrate each of these methods of intervention we provide detailed case studies for discussion.

Cognitive-behavioural type treatment programmes for child sexual abusers

Cognitive-behavioural type programmes – or, to put it at its simplest, educational programmes which focus upon the individual offender's thoughts and behaviour, and the often difficult-to-establish links between the two – have over recent years found favour with treatment professionals in all disciplines (for a well reasoned discussion of the history and efficacy of other treatment approaches, including psycho-dynamic and aversion therapies see Barker and Morgan, 1993). The aim of cognitive-behavioural type sex offender treatment programmes is to convince offenders that those thoughts were wrong which allowed them to behave abusively towards their victims,. The process of intervention is to examine with offenders those of their thoughts, feelings, beliefs, actions and behaviour, which combine to facilitate situations in which they choose to abuse. The methods used to deliver these programmes are quite varied, but are usually involve either; individual sessions, where the abuser works through a set programme of structured objectives with one or two facilitators; or groupwork, which involves several abusers (usually a maximum of eight) working together through identified treatment issues led by professional group work facilitators.

Practitioners preparing to facilitate cognitive-behavioural programmes for child sexual abusers can access an ever increasing number of guidebooks and manuals (for example, Knopp, 1984; Bays & Freeman-Longo, 1989; Eldridge, 1998). While differing somewhat in method and, to a lesser extent, process, these works share a common theoretical foundation: Wolf's sexual assault cycle (1984), and Finkelhor's four preconditions model (1984). Chapters two and three present a more detailed discussion.

In brief, cognitive-behavioural type treatment programmes for child sexual abusers typically consist of the following components:

*   The denial unit, which aims to enable abusers to accept greater responsibility for those behaviours which led them to offend.
*   The offending behaviour unit, which seeks to establish a shared understanding of the abuser's behaviour by identifying key factors which combine to explain, predict and prevent it.
*   The fantasy and arousal unit, which documents the abuser's thoughts and feelings about unlawful sexual behaviour, aiming to direct the offender, as much as is possible, towards either change or control.
*   The distorted cognitions unit, which sets out to help abusers to examine those beliefs and values which impelled them to offend.

- The victim empathy unit, which seeks to educate abusers about their victims experiences.
- The social skills unit, which educates and trains abusers to be more aware of those aspects of their behaviour which are inappropriate, e.g. through anger management and assertiveness training; whilst looking for alternative 'safe' social activities to occupy the abusers' time.
- The relapse prevention unit, documenting the range of thoughts, beliefs, triggers, moods, situations and behaviours which have been identified as contributory factors to the risk of re-offending (more about this later).

To illustrate how these treatment programmes are implemented, we now look at a case example, chosen for the breadth of issues which arise.

Case Study 1: Mick

Mick had been sexually abusing his 10 year old stepdaughter for a period of almost four years. She disclosed the abuse, which involved him rubbing her breasts and genitalia, to a school friend who, in turn, reported it to a schoolteacher. Initially Mick denied the offences but after speaking to his solicitor and realising denial might have resulted in his going to trial, and his stepdaughter having to give evidence, he agreed to admit he had touched her breasts on two occasions.

After several weeks remanded on bail, Mick pleaded guilty to two offences of indecent assault, his plea was accepted on the basis of his admission of touching her breasts on only two occasions. This caused considerable disquiet amongst those professionals not directly involved in the prosecution process. The victim and her family were confused about the decision to accept his plea, and explained they felt as though Mick had managed to fool everybody into believing his stepdaughter had lied to police and social workers.

Mick was convicted of the two offences and the case adjourned for the probation service to prepare a pre-sentence report. He was assessed as suitable for a community treatment programme and entered into a contract with the programme administrators to fully engage in all aspects of the treatment process. The offer of a place on the programme was based on the following conditions:

- that he accepted that a problem existed with his sexual behaviour.
- that he agreed that he needed help to control his behaviour.
- that he agreed there was a great deal more to reveal about his offending.
- that the professionals who assessed him believed he had sufficient genuine motivation to sustain involvement throughout this lengthy and arduous programme.

The court sentences Mick to a three year probation order with conditions, one of which required him to participate in the treatment programme specified. He was obviously relieved not to have been sent to prison, and was able to keep his job at a local factory.

At the time of starting the treatment programme Mick was living at a probation hostel, had no contact with his victim, and was being divorced by his wife. He was not receiving treatment for mental illness nor was he thought to be abusing drugs or alcohol, In many respects he presented as an under-assertive man with low self-esteem. He progressed through the programme units as follows:

Denial

During the denial unit of the programme Mick needed encouragement to talk about the extent of his abusive behaviour. He began to realise the harm he caused the victim and his family, and to acknowledge the planning which had contributed to his abuse of the victim. At times, when he declared he had revealed all that there was to reveal, the treatment facilitators and other group members encouraged him to continue towards a situation where his account of the offending was in close accord with his victim's. Progress was made towards the end of this unit, Mick revealed he had also planned to abuse his stepdaughter's friend on an occasion when she stayed the night at their home. He had entered the room in which the child was sleeping and masturbated himself. He had ejaculated onto the bed in which she was sleeping and took her knickers from the bedroom floor, keeping them to arouse himself when he masturbated and fantasised about her. He had planned to give her several drinks of very strong 'shandy' when she next stayed the night, and then orally abuse her, licking her vagina and ejaculating onto her thighs while she slept. It was clear to the programme workers that Mick had targeted this child as a victim. By the time this unit was completed Mick, and the programme facilitators, had a better understanding of the risk he presented. Mick was left in no doubt about the need for treatment.

Behaviour patterns: Grooming

The next unit of the programme established a better understanding of Mick's offending behaviour, especially the sequence, or chain, of decisions which, in accumulation, constituted the planning of his offences. He identified how he had decided to encourage his wife to join an evening art class, which placed him, on these occasions, in the position of sole carer for her daughter. He then exploited this opportunity as his sexual attraction towards his stepdaughter grew. He further encouraged his wife to socialise with her new friends from the art class, which of course gave him more time alone with his intended victim. Other decisions which Mick identified as relevant to his offending were:

- bathing his stepdaughter,
- taking a shower whilst she was in the bath,
- playfighting with her,
- watching inappropriate films on television with her, e.g. pornography and horror films,
- encouraging her to cuddle him more frequently and to trust him with secrets, thereby creating a closeness which excluded her mother,
- joking with her about the size of her breasts, and the differences between his penis and her vagina,
- blaming her for causing his penis to become erect by looking at it and 'wishing' it to do so,
- making her feel guilty and responsible for the abuse; and
- telling her 'secret' stories of how some girls love to tease penises, and how each girl should be allowed to touch and play with one 'secret' penis; but only if she really wanted to.

At the end of this unit Mick had been able to document how his decisions had led to his abusing his stepdaughter. He could identify high risk situations and the behaviour which led him to commit the offences. Further, as a result, Mick now knew the internal and external triggers which prompted his offending.

Fantasy

The third unit of the programme concentrated on analysing Mick's deviant sexual arousal and fantasies. He learned that his fantasising about young girls led to his sexual arousal, and that the more he fantasised (including masturbation and ejaculation to mental images of them) the more entrenched his sexual attraction became. So, by masturbating to fantasies of touching his stepdaughter he was compounding the problem. Indeed, Mick soon realised that his sexual fantasies were probably what had allowed him to begin to behave in a sexualised way towards her. He was advised to attempt to alter the subject of his fantasies, so rather than imagining he was abusing his stepdaughter, he chose to imagine that he was in the company of an age-appropriate partner. Choosing women as the subject of fantasy, Mick began to experience arousal to women. By the end of this Mick was aware that if he began to fantasise about children again then he was placing himself at risk of re-offending.

Distorted thinking

As Mick entered the fourth unit he was almost half way through the programme, and beginning to feel a little more confident about controlling his behaviour. His wife had divorced him and he still had no contact with his victim. The programme work was now dealing with some of his attitudes and beliefs (often referred to as cognitive distortions) which had influenced his thoughts. Mick soon realised he had misinterpreted the trust and admiration of his stepdaughter as a naive form of sexual attraction. Her innocence, embarrassment and confusion had been translated by Mick as desire and seduction. Here childhood had been re-framed to represent a vulnerable and dependant person with whom he could experience sexual activity. In many respects Mick came to realise that he had disengaged as her parent, seeing himself more as a partner. At the end of this unit Mick realised that his beliefs and attitudes had become entrenched as his abuse of the child continued. He became aware of the significant impact which cognitive distortions can have on abusive behaviour and therefore felt better equipped to reduce the risk of further offending.

Victim empathy

Victim empathy was the focus of the fifth unit, and although Mick engaged well with the tasks set for him, he expressed the view that he had little to learn from this unit as he felt he already had a perfect understanding of how his victim had been affected by the abuse. However, during several of the role reversal exercises Mick broke down, struggling to complete the day's work. He also experienced great difficulty writing a victim apology letter. At the end of this unit Mick acknowledged and described the impact his offending was likely to have had on his stepdaughter.

Social skills

The next unit of the programme helped Mick realise just how isolated he had been at the time the abuse began. He had had no friends, and, other than at work, no adult companionship beyond that of his wife. He also realised he had developed almost chronic under-assertiveness, relying on other people to make important decisions for him. Mick soon became aware that his poor social skills had not helped him to find the strength he needed to avoid offending. Instead, it suited him to develop a closer, intimate relationship with his stepdaughter, as her innocence and naively made him feel important and in control; an experience he had not been able to find while in the company of adults. For Mick, it was somehow easier to impress his stepdaughter than any of the adults he had contact with. This unit helped to equip Mick with the necessary skills and confidence he required to begin to form a wider social network. He was now aware that to withdraw from his peers could once again results in him offending.

Relapse prevention

During the final unit of the programme Mick negotiated a written plan to help him avoid situations which had been identified as 'risky'. This involved being left alone, or seeking situations where he was alone, while looking after children. It also included rehearsed verbal responses to friends or relatives who might, at some stage in the future, ask him to look after children. Mick was also reminded that any fantasies he might develop could lead him to begin once again to target children, especially girls. In addition, his written plan included a list of professional people he could contact in an emergency to seek help. This also included his mother and brother in monitoring his moods and behaviour. By the end of this unit Mick had a clear written framework which documented the do's and don'ts associated with his controlling his behaviour.

Mick completed the programme and was assessed as presenting a medium/high risk of re-offending. In summary each unit had played a part in determining what needed to change to help Mick control his predisposition to abuse:

- Denial. Mick accepted greater responsibility for the nature and extent of his abusive behaviour.
- Behaviour Patterns: Grooming. This unit not only identified how Mick trapped his victim, making her feel partly to blame for the abuse, but also how he had deceived and manipulated his partner.
- Fantasy. Mick accepted that he needed to change his fantasies of young girls to more age-appropriate partners.
- Distorted Thinking. Seeing his stepdaughter as an object of sexual desire Mick had disengaged from his parenting role. Excited by her vulnerability, he misinterpreted her innocence and naivety as sexual attraction,.
- Victim Empathy. Mick found it difficult to accept just how much his victim had suffered as a result of the abuse.
- Social Skills. Lacking the confidence to make the right decisions, Mick had become isolated and under-assertive. He began to broaden his interests and rediscover his self-esteem.
- Relapse Prevention. Mick left the programme with a written plan indicating the key factors relevant to increased risk.

Having completed the programme Mick was able to realise that he would be placing himself at risk of re-offending if he lived in a household with young girls. He remained in touch with the professional agencies which had participated in his treatment.

Effectiveness research:
Do sex offender treatment programmes work?

Child protection, and indeed almost every other system of public service is increasingly subject to review and reorganisation. Policy makers and practitioners are equally keen to implement the methods and approaches which provide the most effective outcomes, at reasonable cost to the public. Accordingly, one of the best ways of making sure of this is to use research evidence to influence service provision. The link between research and policy is not as clear as we might expect, as factors such as expense, ethics, accountability, politics and fashion are never too far from the minds of those who implement change. Quite simply, if you can identify what works from research, then you can be reasonably sure of what you will get from your investment. Effectiveness research is the key to improving the work we do to protect children.

So, let us now examine, albeit briefly, what research can tell us about the effectiveness of cognitive-behavioural sex offender treatment programmes. In doing so we rely on authoritative evidence collected from various well researched projects, instead of electing to patronise claims of efficacy offered in the form of tales of 'wisdom' told by individual practitioners. Child protection research demands more than mere anecdotalism.

In her review of American, and certain rather limited UK cognitive-behavioural programmes, Barker (1996) identified six features of therapeutic programmes for child sexual abusers which have been associated with success. In order to draw together the possible benefits of cognitive-behavioural therapy these six features are discussed below.

1. Types of offender

Careful selection of offenders is required to realise the full potential of these programmes. Rapists are less likely to benefit than child molesters and exhibitionists. The reasons for this are unknown.

Amongst the child molesters receiving treatment, those men who combined more entrenched patterns of sex offending against children, together with seriously inadequate personalities, required longer treatment before change could be observed, than men with less entrenched patterns of behaviour. Careful selection of programme candidates is accordingly advised, not least to target resources more accurately.

2. Length of programme

Longer periods of therapy have been found to be more useful than shorter periods (Ryan, Davis, Miyoshi, Lane and Wilson, 1987). Their research with juvenile child sexual abusers indicated that 9 to 12 months should be the minimum duration of treatment. Unfortunately, no information was given about the delivery of this treatment or how many in total it should include. Barker (1996) cites Fordham (1992) who in the UK found that 'offenders gains' increased over a six month period. This work however does not provide any evidence of its own and is rather speculative regarding the benefits of longer cognitive-behavioural programmes for child sexual abusers. The STEP study (Beckett, Beech, Fisher and Fordham, 1994) found that cognitive-behavioural programmes for child sexual abusers which lasted approximately 60 hours had some success in affecting offenders' attitudes, but the clinicians were unable to implement any relapse prevention safeguards. Short-term programmes were found to have had little or no impact upon entrenched child molesters.. This group were said to be best dealt with in a residential therapeutic environment, to allow for more extensive therapy, though no supporting evidence was advanced. The study also recommended that the entrenched child molesters could be 'monitored' while not being worked with. The suggestion here is of a surveillance function that would presumably involve aspects of external control. In summary, the length of cognitive-behavioural programmes is felt to be associated with success. Other than that of Ryan, Davis, Miyoshi, Lane and Wilson (1987), which appears to have had significant influence on programme development, there is little firm evidence for this view. Overall the principle seems to be no more sophisticated than a view that more of a good thing is better than less.

3. Therapeutic tasks

Ryan and Miyoshi (1990) from the USA reached 'tentative' conclusions about the association of reduced re-offending and therapeutic tasks. They found that, of the offenders who were not re-arrested or questioned about further offending by the police (90.8% of the sample), two such therapeutic gains had been achieved: the ability to identify and interrupt their offence cycle, and to recognise 'triggers' which might act as potentiators to offending. These two therapeutic tasks are fundamental to cognitive-behavioural therapy for child sexual abusers. The recognition of these features associated with the success of cognitive-behavioural programmes is arguably quite significant. It indicates, albeit in a very small sample of 69 American juvenile child sexual abusers, a common element associated with those who have seemingly conformed and managed to use self-control.

4. Impressions of success in therapy

Effectiveness is of fundamental importance to workers, but Ryan and Miyoshi (1990) discovered that clinicians could not accurately predict which of the child sexual abusers receiving therapy would re-offend. This had obvious implication for the value of expert opinion in risk assessments, and indicated that because professional opinion is not a reliable source of offence predictions there exists a need for the development of an objective risk assessment instrument to aid professional judgement such as those referred to earlier in chapter 5. This, however, does not tell us anything about the success of cognitive-behavioural therapies, informing us only of the limitations of those whose job it is to deliver them.

5. Relapse prevention

Relapse prevention is universally regarded as an essential part of any cognitive-behavioural programme (Marques, Day, Nelson, Miner and West, 1991; Pithers, 1990; Beckett, Beech, Fisher and Fordham, 1994) which consolidates and maintains therapeutic changes. The American Sex Offender Treatment Evaluation Project (SOTEP) cited by Barker (1996) revealed that the strongest predictor of re-offending was the offender's ability to apply relapse prevention skills learnt in the programme; suggesting that imparting a sense of responsibility for offending behaviour was not alone enough to lower the risk of recidivism. Relapse prevention is that part of a cognitive-behavioural programme which deals with concrete action as opposed to abstract thinking about the offending. Avoidance of risky, offence-specific situations is encouraged to enable child sexual abusers to benefit from personal, professional and community surveillance. In relapse prevention work the opportunities for offending are reduced and the chances of detection are increased. The opportunities to develop this type of intervention even further are discussed later.

It is worthy of note that the research used as evidence for the value of relapse prevention by Barker is that of Pithers (1990) who demonstrated a 4% re-conviction rate from a four year follow up study of 167 child molesters and rapists. This impressive result arises from using programmes which focus on both motivation and opportunity.

6. Programme implementation and management

As one would expect, it seems that better organised and task-centred programmes which pursue group and individual supervision plans, and tend to demonstrate good group cohesion are most effective (Stephenson, 1991; Beckett, Barker, Beech, Fisher and Fordham, 1994). Cognitive-behavioural treatment programmes for child sexual abusers are held in surprisingly high regard by managers and practitioners in the probation and prison services. Optimism as to their potential value exists despite a general lack of research findings to measure their impact on re-offending. It does appear, however, that some, less entrenched child molesters, respond better than more entrenched child molesters and rapists; that longer term programmes are more effective than shorter ones; that offence cycle specific components and relapse prevention initiatives are beneficial; and that good management and task-centred delivery are important. Relapse prevention and its association with opportunity reduction and improved detection rates are issues to be pursued further. In this summary of the perceived benefits of cognitive-behavioural programmes aimed at sex offenders, it is worthy of note that support exists for the role of monitoring and surveillance. In fact the most impressive results emerge from programmes which use external control methods (see for example Pithers, 1990).

Relapse prevention with child sexual abusers

Relapse prevention involves treatment utilising varying degrees of surveillance. It represents an ethically unproblematic method of supervision because it is predominantly treatment focused and could not work without taking a therapeutic lead. We have already seen that relapse prevention is considered essential to programme integrity but remains grossly underdeveloped so: what does relapse prevention have to offer? and can we identify the elements which set it apart from treatment-only initiatives? Having done this we must then see if there is evidence that it works.

Cognitive-behavioural programmes offer very little in the way of surveillance or monitoring to control offending. Later in this chapter we will discuss the case of Charlie, and see how his inability to self report issues relating to risk led him to plan further offending. The abuser's dereliction of responsibility is invisible to treatment facilitators, although it remains implicit to all of those professionals dealing with risk.

Surveillance is the only way to monitor whether there is true motivation to refrain from re-offending. Many practitioners do not recognise this as a task which should involve them, and have resisted moves to introduce more intrusive methods of intervention. For simplification of this issue, it may be helpful for us to view intervention, in a general sense, as consisting of internal and external dimensions While to separate these two factors for the purpose of analysis might be thought to create an opportunity for comparison, such comparison would not provide the answers we seek at this point. External and internal dimensions of intervention are more productively viewed as complementary halves which together can be combined to produce a whole greater than the sum of the parts. This potential is not always realised by practitioners, who may concentrate on the internal dimension of intervention by means such as counselling, treatment, advice giving and social work support.

The external dimension which involves active surveillance of the offender's involvement with his environment is becoming increasingly important. The overlap of these two dimensions is, as we have seen, often referred to as relapse prevention (RP) and is identified as an essential aspect to current treatment strategies (Beckett, Beech, Fisher and Fordham, 1994). The development of RP initiatives is discussed later; for the moment it is the external dimension of intervention, which rests comfortably in the sex offending models of Finkelhor and Wolf, upon which we shall focus.

Carey and McGrath (1989) provide an insightful starting position for us to begin to look at some of the possibilities for the surveillance. In their article, which adopts a very clear treatment perspective, they argue that manipulation of a sex offender's environment to limit his access to 'external stimulus cues', and to find alternative uses for his time, will impact to reduce the urge to offend and also enhance the efficacy of other control methods. Using the term 'environmental interventions' they argue that offenders will experience considerable difficulty in responding to treatment if their environment remains unchanged. Equally, maintaining any treatment changes will prove difficult if not reinforced with environmental change.

Taking a strong lead from earlier work with alcoholics, environmental intervention broadens the scope for traditional, individual centred work and includes changes in social contingencies. Family, employment and social interaction which encourage or discourage the problem behaviour is the focus of attention. Increasing family and community awareness of supervision aims can create a method of surveillance. If this method of supervision has anything to offer sex offender treatment then it may include, for example, meeting with close family and friends to discuss the aims of treatment and inform them of the assessed degree of risk, restricting employment opportunities to reduce the likelihood of the offender obtaining access to potential victims, and monitoring social and leisure pursuits to facilitate constructive and appropriate use of time that does not present opportunities for offending. It is not enough to limit the arena for change to therapy sessions. Stimulus, opportunity and victims are rarely found in the treatment room (although this should never be ruled out completely of course). The offender's interaction with his environment requires our consideration also.

Marques and Nelson (1989, p.37) argue the importance of

locating environmental high-risk elements. They define these as situational or behavioural events which increase the chances of a sexual offence by providing the cues and contingencies for illicit sexual behaviour. The authors cite Mischel (1973); a proponent of social learning theory, who defines important external or situational variables as those which provide information influencing an individual's expectations, constructions, motivations, evaluations of stimuli, or ability to generate responses. Environmental high risk elements for sex offending are those that can be shown to influence relapse. The most obvious environmental high risk element is the presence of a potential victim. The chances of re-offending if a necrophiliac starts work as an undertaker's assistant, or a child rapist frequents swimming baths during school sessions, will be considerably increased. Contact with potential victims needs to be considered and manipulated by external control.

It is not reasonable to suggest that all contact with all potential victims should be avoided. Striving to argue for such a goal attracts criticism from civil libertarians who regard such a position as too oppressive and restrictive, though this need not deter us from exploring the full potential of environmental interventions with a view to managing identified risk. To review the full extent of environmental risk factors is too exhaustive for our present discussion. It is enough to acknowledge that a wide range of possible situational variables must be considered and their relevance for a given offender determined by analysis of the conditions surrounding his particular crimes. To achieve this the relationship between internal and external dimensions of supervision has to be based upon a thorough appreciation of their combined value.

Relapse prevention as mentioned earlier is the process of maintaining change in order to prevent offending. It was originally devised as a method to help substance misusers refrain from problem behaviour. Chaney, O'Leary and Marlatt (1987) described how relapse prevention was designed to strengthen self-control by facilitating the identification of problematic situations, analysing decisions which contribute to the problem and developing strategies to avoid these situations, or cope more effectively with them. Relapse prevention is therefore a functional hybrid of external and internal supervision which emerged from the development of self-management skills. The emphasis remains on internal strengths but places them, with common-sense practicality, within the person's everyday life situations. A shift from internal to external, from individual to environmental, reportedly emerged. Pithers, Marques, Gibat and Marlatt (1983) modified the self-management model of relapse prevention for application to child sexual abusers.

Pithers (1990, p.357) argues that attention must be paid to the capacity of child sexual abusers to fail in attempts to self-manage their behaviour. They may neglect to employ the safeguards suggested and a lapse may occur that would not be reported to the therapist. In his work at the Vermont Treatment Programme for Child Sexual Abusers, Pithers found that despite the granting of immunity from punitive consequences for a lapse reported to the therapist, the tendency has been for secrecy to remain, and so the internal self-management dimension of relapse prevention was sometimes inadequate. In view of this he developed a new dimension of relapse prevention for child sexual abusers.

Pithers and his colleagues in Vermont set out to develop a more comprehensive programme. To compensate for the shortcomings of the internal dimension they focused on external methods to enhance community safety. Gaining access to accurate information about the sex offender was considered essential, any possible lapses or problematic behaviour needing to be known by therapist and supervising officer. This led to the development of the external supervisory dimension of relapse prevention (Pithers, Buell, Kashima, Cumming and Beal, 1987; Pithers, Cumming, Beal, Young and Turner, 1989). Surveillance is a feature of this development. Pithers (1990) identifies three functions of the external supervisory dimension:

1. Enhancing efficacy of supervision by monitoring the abuser's behaviour (specific offence precursors).
2. Increasing the efficacy of supervision by creating an informed network of familial contacts which assists practitioners in monitoring the child sexual abusers behaviour.
3. Creating a collaborative relationship with professionals conducting therapy with the abuser.

Monitoring behaviour

The first of these three functions is to establish offence precursors or elements of behaviour which are clearly related to the individual's risk of subsequent offending. We could also refer to these as offence indicators or dynamic risk variables. As it is neither possible nor necessary to monitor all the offender's behaviour, there is concentration on certain aspects, the offence precursors. When detected, the offence precursor informs the supervising officer of the imminence of relapse and appropriate action can be taken to intervene. A risk assessment and ongoing therapy are the best source of information from which to determine these precursors.

Family and community support

The second is the use of collateral contacts. These are identified people known to the offender who act to support the maintenance of self-management. They are informed of the risk variables, or offence precursors, and act as tripwires to prevent further offending. These collateral contacts include people such as friends, family, neighbours, and employers. They are encouraged to report lapses to the supervising practitioner. Regular meetings and communication help reinforce the network of community support.

Networking

The third function involves liaison between the child protection professionals and programme facilitators who provide treatment for the offender. Progress and problems can be discussed and alternative interventions arranged. The work of Pithers and his various collaborators in the 1980s has parallels with the much earlier work of Shaw (1973) in Southend, who, though he did not report on his work in great detail, is a forerunner of these more detailed developments in the United States.

Surveillance of child sexual abusers is not of course the sole responsibility of any one agency. Many organisations pursue this activity as and we have already seen. Opportunities for surveillance can enhance therapeutic work. Relapse prevention has extended this capacity, first by aiming to improve offenders self-management skills and also by involving external agents in monitoring behaviour. Relapse prevention is a method of working with child sexual abusers which requires practitioners to make use of certain aspects of community and professional surveillance. It has been demonstrated to be effective in reducing recidivism. There is scope, however, to develop relapse prevention further, and to do so represents a natural development from the current position. However, it is debatable whether the term relapse prevention will remain appropriate. Linking together the shared principles of situational crime prevention and relapse prevention produces an opportunity to appreciate the separate advantages of each. A more correct name for such a method may be 'Risk Management'. This does not assume that we are working with an offender who has stopped offending, as the word 'relapse' suggests, nor does it carry the connotation of being solely a therapeutic activity. Risk management as a generic term invites and encourages the equal participation of agencies with shared interests and one common goal—the prevention of offending.

Controlling child sexual abusers in the community: Multi-agency risk management

We have seen how treatment, in some instances, can provide opportunities for child sexual abusers to alter their behaviour through internal control. We have also looked at how additional safeguards can be implemented through relapse prevention initiatives, which use various methods of surveillance to enhance public safety. Risk management initiatives are now legislated for in the Sex Offender Act 1997. Throughout England and Wales the police have emerged as lead agency, hosting public protection meetings, at which individual child sexual abusers are assessed and discussed. As yet there are few examples of how risk management practice is defined, let alone coordinated; though for two such examples see Kemshall (1996), and Grant (1998). The former for a thorough examination of risk culture in public services, the latter for the research and development of a new model for community supervision of child sexual abusers; the Sex Offender Risk Management Approach (SORMA).

Using a case example, let us now examine how multi-agency risk management of child sexual abusers can be implemented.

Case Study 2: Charlie

At 50 years of age Charlie, a retired school teacher, was due for release from prison after serving 4 years for indecency offences, including attempted rape, gross indecency, indecent assault and taking indecent photographs; all against boys aged between 6 and 9 years. Although Charlie had no previous convictions, it was established that his offending had been a long term problem, reaching back 20 years or more. Charlie accepted he would need help to control his behaviour once released.

During his prison sentence Charlie participated in a sex offender treatment programme. It was believed he had made good progress; having impressed the programme facilitators with his ability to absorb the educational elements of the programme very quickly. He learned the jargon and found it easy to understand the issues discussed. Charlie was keen to please, and never displayed intolerance, boredom or frustration for fear of being considered rude. His true feelings were never witnessed on the programme. Charlie was bright enough to know what the course facilitators wanted, and provided this to ensure they regarded him in the most positive way possible.

Although none of the professionals were aware at the time, Charlie yearned to be released so he could resume his abusive relationship with Andrew, an 11 year old accommodated in a local authority residential unit near to the area in which Charlie had lived. He had kept a photograph of Andrew in his prison cell, and possessed a vast collection of indecent photographs and video recordings of Andrew and several other boys of a similar age, in an attic bedroom of his sister's home which he had used as a meeting place with boys. Charlie had never divulged the whereabouts, or even existence of this secret store, but he knew he desperately wanted to be there with Andrew and his young friends.

Charlie's probation officer was unfamiliar to the case, although she knew that previous officers had assessed him as presenting a high risk of re-offending. She also knew he had completed a sex offender programme within the confines of the prison, and was believed to have made good progress. The probation officer's task was to protect the public by rehabilitating Charlie: a very difficult but nevertheless common situation for probation officers, particularly those who work exclusively with child sexual abusers. Such work requires a dual focus, and the often unavoidable tendency is to compromise one area of responsibility to make progress in the other.

The cognitive-behavioural sex offender programme Charlie had completed equipped him with a range of strategies to avoid offending; provided of course he chose to implement them. Further to this, Charlie also had a written relapse prevention plan, compiled with help from his course facilitators. In brief, his relapse prevention plan was as follows:

Charlie's Relapse Prevention Plan

Risky feelings:	Loneliness/isolation
	No one cares
	I'm worthless
	I'm bored
	I need comfort
Risky thoughts:	I won't get caught
	Just one more offence won't matter
	I won't harm anyone
	I really can't resist the urge
	I deserve to feel good
	The boy will love and respect me.
Risky behaviours:	Drinking alcohol
	Going for long walks
	Going for long drives
	Watching schoolboy football
	Masturbating to fantasies of boys
	Befriending boys
	Possessing child pornography
	Using children's internet chat/news forums,
	Pretending to be a boy

Risky situations: Being alone with boys
       Offering tutoring
       Photographing boys
       Allowing boys to ride in my car
       Visiting amusements arcades with a pocketful
       of change
       Using public transport at school times, i.e.
       8.15-9.00am and 3.00-5.00pm
       Talking to boys in public toilets.

Who to contact in emergencies:
       My probation officer
       local police
       my sister Elsie
       my doctor
       my church leader.

Just prior to his release to a probation hostel, Charlie's probation officer held a multi-agency risk management meeting at the prison. She decided to approach her task of protecting the public from Charlie by sharing what information she had about him with other practitioners and managers with a legitimate interest. Taking the view she was the person best placed to coordinate a multi-agency risk management plan, and having a statutory duty to supervise Charlie, she agreed to chair the meeting and prepare a brief written report for the other professionals present. These were:

Principal social worker in child protection - SSD
Area social worker - SSD
Hostel manager - probation service
Detective inspector - police
Detective constable - police
Area officer - prison service
Programme facilitator - prison service
Personal officer - prison service.

The meeting lasted an hour with Charlie attending for approximately half that time. It opened with a brief verbal report from the sex offender programme facilitator who summarised the work Charlie had done. Charlie was asked if he wanted to comment on the report. He chose to explain how useful it had all been, equipping him with enough insight and control to avoid re-offending. The police officer asked Charlie what level of risk he presented, to which he replied 'medium'. He then went on to explain why he thought this; which introduced many issues relating to the work he completed on the programme.

The social worker was interested to learn of any children in his extended family who he might, at some stage, have contact with. Charlie explained that his only living relative was his sister, Elsie, who worked abroad as a nurse for 6 months every year. She had no children and lived alone in the home their parents had owned, which Charlie looked after while she was away.

The personal officer at the prison described how Charlie was somewhat of a loner, preferring to spend time alone in his cell, in which he had very few personal items of property. The officer remembered an occasion when Charlie was disciplined for becoming verbally abusive towards another prisoner, seemingly because he removed a photograph from Charlie's cell as a prank.

Charlie was thanked for his cooperation in the meeting and then escorted back to his wing whilst the professionals remained to negotiate a risk management plan. The probation officer commented that she had been impressed by the way Charlie conducted himself in the meeting, seeming only to get uncomfortable when his personal officer had mentioned the discipline matter.

The personal officer then explained how he was rather puzzled about the photograph, having heard Charlie say he had no relatives other than Elsie. He remembered Charlie telling him the photograph was of Andrew, his nephew, who was 11 years old. Charlie had also telephoned Andrew from the prison on at least 2 occasions he was aware of. Understandably there was a sense of concern over Charlie's contact with this boy.

The area police officer was interested to know where Elsie's house was, and whether anyone had ever visited it. The probation officer remembered reading in Charlie's file that he had been bailed to reside with a relative after first appearing in court. She checked her file and gave the addresses to the police and social workers. The meeting then made the following recommendations:

1. That the personal officer would photocopy the photograph of Andrew and send this to the police and social worker. It was agreed Charlie should not be made aware of the expressed concern, as he was considered unlikely to tell the truth about the boy's identity, and to destroy the photograph.
2. That the hostel impose a rule requiring Charlie to complete a movement chart every morning logging the places he was due to visit that day.
3. That the hostel manager inform the police of the registration number of any vehicle Charlie becomes the keeper of.
4. That Charlie be instructed not to communicate or associate with any person under the age of 16 years.
5. That a condition be placed on his licence preventing him from engaging in any employment or activity which brought him into direct contact with children.
6. That the risk management meeting re-convene in 3 months.

Charlie was unaware of the concern expressed about him at the risk management meeting. He believed that his progress on the sex offender programme had been so remarkable as to overwhelm the professionals, reducing any fears they might have had that he could re-offend.

Within two weeks of his release from prison Charlie had been re-arrested. The photograph, which had been passed to the social worker, had in turn been shown to colleagues and other staff in the hope of a positive identification. A residential social worker recognised Andrew as a child they looked after. The staff at the home were concerned for him and discovered he was having contact with Charlie, who had bought him a new pair of trainers and arranged for him to spend an afternoon at Elsie's House. The social worker reported this to Charlie's probation officer who coordinated a response from the hostel and police. Charlie completed the hostel movement chart with false information; declaring he would be at the public library. The police followed Charlie to Elsie's and then knocked on the door at the time Andrews was expected.

As Charlie opened the door he was arrested for breaching his licence conditions: Andrew had given a statement to the police that he had been having contact with Charlie. The arrest provided an opportunity for police to search the house for anything which might incriminate him. The police soon discovered Charlie's stash of child pornography and a series of diaries containing detailed descriptions of offences committed against other boys. Charlie was later convicted of child abduction, rape, gross indecency, indecent assault, and possessing indecent photographs.

The risk management initiative had proved successful. Charlie had been given every opportunity to address his behaviour using internal control. He had even been issued with a written relapse prevention plan. However, his motivation to refrain from offending had not sufficiently diminished the urge for sexual gratification and emotional satisfaction. Although he had understood the programme and provided all the right answers, he chose to re-offend almost immediately.

In summary, the following attempts had been made to prevent Charlie from re-offending:

• A cognitive-behavioural type treatment programme had provided the first opportunity for him to learn to control his behaviour.
• A relapse prevention plan had detailed how Charlie could avoid situations in which the risk of re-offending was increased.
• Finally, the risk management initiative, which does not rely on internal methods of control detected Charlie's offending, and in so doing helped to identify victims in need of therapy.

External methods of control can prove essential in child protection initiatives because they place less dependency on the hope that offenders will control their own behaviour.

Intervening without statutory authority: Working with unconvicted child sexual abusers

Relatively few sexual abusers are successfully prosecuted or made subject to a finding of fact in civil proceedings. In view of this practitioners are beginning to experiment with methods of intervention with child sexual abusers who have not been identified in legal proceedings but where there exists an identified need to assess, treat, monitor, and in some cases, contain their behaviour. It stands to reason that time and effort spent on providing a service to this majority group, is a worthwhile investment; for this is where the need is greatest.

Traditionally, treatment providers have peddled the notion that without legal mandate child sexual abusers would be unlikely to cooperate with, or even attend, a cognitive-behavioural type treatment programme; an experience which most child sexual abusers are believed to find so distasteful they would rather avoid. We can understand why such 'wisdom' emerged, although a critical appraisal of the quest for credence in cognitive-behavioural treatment of child sexual abusers is not our present concern. Treatment is usually perceived as a 'soft option' and the need to demonstrate efficacy has impeded confidence in and development of this work, the political climate having become less than sympathetic towards rehabilitative supervision in recent years.

So, is it possible to engage unconvicted child sexual abusers in cognitive-behavioural type programmes, or not? And if it is, what are the chances of it working?

There is, as yet, no research to help answer these questions. However, if we compare these two groups of offenders: men who are convicted, and those who are not; we can see very little difference. In fact there have been no differences reported in any of the current literature on the subject.

Responsibility and motivation are two of the most important factors which determine an abuser's success in completing a treatment programme. These are major issues which emerge from all types of treatment, supervision and rehabilitative interventions; not just those which deal with child sexual abusers. From this position we could speculate that if an abuser appreciates that his behaviour is a problem, and one for which he seeks help, then perhaps he is accepting enough responsibility to warrant intervention. Providing help in such a scenario is certainly preferable to not helping. If the child sexual abuser is unable to accept responsibility for a certain act, for example where a victim alleges a specified offence; then we must ask the question of whether or not his acceptance of general, rather than specific, responsibility is enough to deem him suitable for treatment. Complete, absolute and unfaltering responsibility is never likely to be found intact in child sexual abusers at this stage of assessment. It may even be possible for an unconvicted child sexual abuser to accept a greater sense of responsibility than a convicted offender, whose admission of a certain act is as much as he is willing to disclose. For child sexual abusers who have not been convicted there remains an additional ethical dilemma: should any admission in treatment become the subject of arrest and prosecution? Or should such a decision remain at the discretion of the treatment facilitators?

The second of these issues; the offender's motivation to receive help, can be gauged at a number of levels: First, what the offender has to say about wanting help. Secondly, by identifying what it is that he wants to achieve by receiving help. Thirdly, exploring what he stands to lose by not receiving help; and last, examining what is revealed through other sources to indicate his motivation to seek help. If his motivation is clear and thought to be substantial enough to see him through a complete programme, then, provided he seeks help for the right reasons, he might well engage favourably with an appropriate programme.

The following case example is used here to illustrate some of the issues which might arise in the course of professional intervention with a family where child sexual abuse is disclosed:

Case Study 3: Ron

Ron's 14 year old stepdaughter complained to a school friend that Ron had indecently assaulted her on two occasions whilst her mother was out shopping. She gave a detailed statement to the police describing how he had touched her breasts and buttocks whilst she stood at the kitchen sink in her nightie. There was no forensic or corroborative evidence to support her allegation, which Ron was advised by his solicitor to deny. He was charged and bailed to reside at an address 10 miles from his home.

Ron's wife was unsure who to believe. She supported her daughter as best she could but still loved Ron, finding it very difficult to believe he could have done such a thing. She and Ron had two younger daughters who both lived at home, and who soon began to miss their father, increasing the dilemma for Ron's wife.

At the initial child protection conference the police indicated that they doubted that the matter could be proceeded with by the Crown Prosecution Service, nevertheless a comprehensive file was being prepared and would be submitted for a decision. The social worker expressed concern over the risk of abuse to all three girls, which was echoed throughout the conference. One of the recommendations of the conference was that a comprehensive social work assessment should be conducted. Ron and his wife were very cooperative during the assessment. Although he denied the offence, he accepted he had recently found himself sexually attracted to his stepdaughter, a matter which initially was very difficult for his wife to accept. Further on in the assessment Ron acknowledged that a problem existed, even though he still denied the charge he requested help to control his behaviour. He realised his denial raised certain doubts about his stepdaughter's honesty, and although it hurt him to think of this, he could not admit to the offence.

The comprehensive assessment was completed in 10 weeks, by which time the police had been notified that the prosecution file had been rejected on the grounds it was unlikely to be successful in the absence of forensic or corroborative evidence.

Ron wanted to return home to his wife and family, who had all expressed a desire for him to do so. His bail ended when the charges were withdrawn; yet they agreed to live apart pending the outcome of a scheduled child protection review conference.

Ron and his wife fully understood the concerns of the professionals, agreeing to do whatever they could to cooperate. The shared focus of concern was Ron's behaviour, and at the review conference it was agreed he would participate in a cognitive-behavioural treatment programme before a final decision was made to support re-unification. The possibility of one day being able to return home was a great motivational influence for Ron.

During the cognitive-behavioural programme, conducted by a multi-agency team, Ron engaged in the full range of units covering all of the issues. He has never admitted the offences he had been charged with; but accepted responsibility for sexually abusive behaviour towards his stepdaughter. In the review at the end of the cognitive-behavioural programme Ron was assessed as having made good progress. He had compiled a relapse prevention plan prior to his return, which was 18 months after he first left. Ron's family also benefited from counselling which had addressed self protection issues, and had been well prepared for his eventual return home.

Conclusion

Cognitive-behavioural programmes for child sexual abusers offer some convicted offenders the opportunity to examine and control their behaviour. Selected research of the efficacy of this type of intervention has prompted considerable optimism amongst practitioners, policy makers and some academics, resulting in cautious exploration and resourcing of such treatment programmes. Accordingly, these programmes are currently popular. Relapse prevention has emerged as the one element of cognitive-behavioural type treatment programmes most associated with success. The likely reason for this is that relapse prevention relies on external, as well as internal, methods of control; often providing confirmation from sources more reliable than the abuser himself, that treatment gains (modified behaviour) are maintained. Risk management of child sexual abusers, particularly public protection models such as the Sex Offender Risk Management Approach (SORMA) referred to earlier, combines treatment initiatives with the structures of multi-agency surveillance, assessment and crime prevention. This comprehensive approach to child protection finds a comfortable habitation within a multi-agency arena.

We have also looked, briefly, at extending the arm of professional guidance beyond those abusers with convictions. Some of the progress and achievements experienced with convicted abusers can stimulate new developments in work with those who are not. And as we have seen, these are the majority.

Finally, we have suggested there is a desperate need for more objective research into methods of intervention with child sexual abusers. Effectiveness research is vital in all areas of public protection; indeed, it is difficult to imagine how progress could ever be made without it.

Chapter 9

Techniques in supervision for those working with sexual abusers

Clark Baim

If you have come to help me, you are wasting your time. But if you have come because your liberation is bound up with mine, then let us work together. (Words of an aboriginal Australian woman quoted in Hudgins, 1998)

Introduction

The idea of supervision often conjures an image of a clinical space, with an external professional offering expert guidance and uninterrupted time to reflect on practice. However, for many practitioners this is far from the reality; in many cases, supervision is erratically provided or neglected altogether. This may be due to the common conception that supervision is a low priority for those who already possess expertise in their field, or because supervision is considered too time consuming, expensive or even off limits for non-specialists unless an external supervisor is called in.

Yet supervision need not be considered the exclusive domain of the expert, as if it were hidden behind mists of arcane wisdom.

On the contrary, supervision can be practised far more broadly and in a much more straightforward fashion than many perceive. Supervision can be conducted among co-workers, in peer groups and among peer networks, as well as through the use of an outside specialist supervisor. Where options are limited, self-supervision is also an option for the individual practitioner. It is a mistake to assume that in order to be done correctly supervision must be facilitated by an objective third party. While this may be an ideal to work toward, there are still many benefits to be gained from conducting supervision in these other ways. Supervision should be seen as an everyday, 'grass roots' activity, something that workers can do to help themselves immediately, with or without outside assistance.

Supervision in working with abusers

As the quotation at the start of the chapter reminds us, the process of therapy, counselling or groupwork inevitably impacts on the lives of both the helper and the helped. Among other benefits, supervision provides a way of acknowledging this inevitability and understanding the significance of the impact. As Geraldine Swain (1995) writes:

Any one of us looking back at the human pain and social distress ... to which we have been exposed - not to mention our own - must surely question what makes us suppose we can practice effectively without ... a regular, conscientious examination of our work, of what might improve it and what impedes it, and of our own feelings about it. (p.12)

As those working in the field will know, there are few areas in counselling or groupwork more likely to lead to worker burn-out or unethical practice than work with sex offenders. Consequently there are many issues, both personal and professional, for workers to address when reflecting on their work with abusers.

Typical issues that impact on workers include emotional overload; fear and revulsion when listening to offence descriptions; confusion about one's own sexual history and attractions; concern about incidents in one's own life that may have been abusive;

concern or confusion about feelings of sexual arousal during sessions and concern about feeling like a voyeur; lack of sexual interest in one's own private life; concern about becoming part of an abuser's fantasies; recognising and coming to terms with our own potential to abuse and our 'internal predator'; persecution tendencies that result from anger at abusers; concern about personal safety; concern about 'catching' abusive behaviour as one would catch a disease; hyper-vigilance – seeing abuse 'everywhere'; revulsion at and rejection of one's professional field by colleagues, family and friends; and the depression, isolation, stagnation, trauma and burn-out that can result from all of the above.

For professionals working with abusers, addressing these issues through adequate supervision is essential not just for one's emotional well-being, but also to ensure the effectiveness and ethical integrity of programme delivery. Equally, supervision encourages an organisation to consider practitioners as whole individuals who have thoughts and feelings as well as a functional role, and who have, under the right circumstances, the ability to grow and improve as professionals (Morrison, 1995). In this light, supervision can be seen as a golden opportunity for training and development.

Among colleagues, supervision can open up taboo or difficult areas for discussion and encourage honest and open communication that promotes reflective practice and constructive critique. Team supervision assists colleagues in coming to a common understanding of sexual aggression and the professional stance they will take with offenders. For example, how will they balance the need for rapport with the need to challenge exploitative beliefs? How will they handle overtly sexist or racist remarks? What assumptions will they make about the offender, his behaviour patterns and his history of offending? How will they support each other in the session?

Colleagues also need to discuss and become sensitive to their own and each other's beliefs regarding sexuality, gender, power, privilege and the social history of gender politics, and how these factors form the context of sexual aggression. Furthermore, colleagues need to share and develop together their understanding of what approaches work best in sex offender treatment. Without coming to a common understanding of these issues, colleagues will be severely restricted in their communication with and trust in each other. Offenders can discern this and will often, in the interests of self- protection, sabotage the session by arguing points, playing one leader off against the other, or simply refusing to cooperate.

If we accept the notion that the client can only progress with you as far as you yourself have progressed, it should become clear that a worker facing burn out and depression, denying their own feelings, deeply mired in confusion and anger, or in conflict with their colleagues, will have limited ability to perform their role. Furthermore, colleagues who are unable to discuss feelings in front of each other, or who avoid doing so, should not be surprised if the offenders in their sessions are making little progress or are becoming rebellious and critical of the programme.

About the techniques described here

This chapter offers six straightforward techniques for supervision that are based on widely used psychodramatic action methods such as role reversal, the empty chair, doubling ('thought bubble') techniques and role play (Blatner, 1973). They are techniques involving some movement and imagination, as this is often a preferred method of doing supervision (Houston, 1990, p.62).

The techniques have been designed so that they can be facilitated when alone, in pairs or in a group, with or without an outside supervisor. They apply as well to work with individuals as with groups. The techniques do not demand specialist knowledge or skills from the facilitator of the supervision, other than basic skills in group leadership and sensitivity to the needs and feelings of those involved. They can be used by non-specialists as long as those involved are willing to be warm, genuine, respectful and tolerant of each other and the facilitator.

Some of these techniques were developed in direct work with offenders. The reader should feel free to adapt and apply the techniques to their own practice. Those interested in the further application of psychodramatic or action methods in groupwork with sex offenders are encouraged to read Jefferies (1991 and 1996).

Structuring supervision:
Content, process and feelings

The context of supervision varies depending upon the demands, working arrangements or practical possibilities that exist within each work setting. Few agencies specify the relationship between the quantity of supervision that is expected of workers in relation to caseload or group sessions. Therefore it is frequently left to the discretion of managers and practitioners to negotiate a level of supervision that meets the workers' needs and provides adequate support and training. For some, this might translate into weekly meetings, for others, supervision will be less frequent.

When structuring supervision sessions, it may be helpful to use a standard format that will help ensure that the key areas of practice are addressed consistently. The following three-step format, covering content, underlying processes and feelings may act as a useful guide. The three steps do not need to be done in sequence, but should rather be borne in mind when considering aspects of practice.

Addressing the content

In addressing the content of a session, one is examining the overt behaviour of all those present in the session. The focus is on what was said, how those present behaved, how information was conveyed, how people interacted, and how the structure of the session was maintained. Critical moments from the group can be examined and magnified. Consideration can be given to how successfully any particular material may have been conveyed in the session, and what methods or strategies might improve delivery of the content.

Techniques two and six may be particularly useful when looking at the content of a session.

Addressing the underlying processes

Consideration of the underlying processes in the session draws focus upon the hidden dynamics. Underlying conflicts, preoccupations and group themes can be highlighted (e.g. the theme of mistrust, or the theme of feeling persecuted or helpless). Paying attention to these 'sub-textual' forces helps to deal with dynamics in a direct way and encourages the practitioner to assess the impact of these forces on their professional functioning. For example, it is useful to identify and deal with the worker's own feelings toward clients and to pin point any parallel process (or unconscious dynamics) existing within supervision and between the worker and the client(s) (Hawkins and Shohet, 1989).

To use another common example, it may be that the worker has highly persecutory thoughts or even feelings of hatred toward the abuser and is highly critical of the abuser's seeming lack of commitment, his slow progress or his distorted beliefs. The worker may feel the need to prove their own expertise by getting 'results' and trying to 'force' the offender to feel certain feelings or to change (Blatner, 1973). It may be useful to consider whether the worker's feelings are reflective of what others have felt about this offender. It may be that this is an old pattern of interaction for the offender, perhaps one that began in childhood. Given this, it is vitally important for the worker to avoid falling into the trap of pushing or coercing the offender, thereby repeating the age-old patterns which may result in the worker re-abusing the abuser - a deeply unethical practice that has elsewhere been termed 'legitimised nonce-bashing' (Sheath, 1990) and which has historically been a source of the worst practices seen in sex offender treatment.

Techniques number one, four and five may be particularly useful in addressing underlying processes. Technique two may also be useful in addressing underlying issues between co-workers.

Addressing worker feelings

It is important to allow time to identify and discuss feelings one has during sessions, and the feelings one is left with. In particular, it is important to discuss negative feelings such as powerlessness, despair, or vengefulness. If these feelings are not discussed and processed fully in an understanding and non-judgmental context, the practitioner can be left feeling unsupported, isolated and de-skilled. The risk is that these feelings may be vented in inappropriate ways, in or out of session, or lead to destructive behaviour and a callous attitude toward abusers. On the other hand, as Swain (p.95) reminds us, '[self-understanding of] our own vulnerability can be one of our strongest assets.'

Techniques number one and especially three may be most useful in addressing workers' feelings.

Points of caution

1. It is essential to allow the staff plenty of time to de-brief after using these techniques, to process what they have learned, to share feedback and insights they gained from being in role, and to speak about their feelings.
2. These techniques may raise vulnerable personal issues for those involved. If those involved in the supervision feel safe enough, they may wish to make reference to deeper and more vulnerable issues, but this is certainly not required in a staff supervision context. However, what emerges in supervision may point to a need for a worker to do further personal work, and if this is the case they should be encouraged to do so in another setting. Methods such as these are best suited to those settings where individual counselling, therapy or clinical supervision are available options when needed.
3. Role plays often serve to unleash surprising levels of boisterousness, and staff can sometimes be disturbed at how far 'over the top' they go almost without thinking about it. It is often a matter of getting carried away by the role, and the spontaneity of the role play. It is right that supervision should bring a measure of lightness and spontaneity to the work. We should allow ourselves to speak freely about our concerns, our 'gut reactions,' our horror, our disgust, and even our macabre sense of humour. Far from being destructive, airing these 'naughty' thoughts or 'unprofessional' feelings is a very healthy process, as long as this is used constructively in the service of improved practice, and without a burden of guilt or fear of censorship. When role players get carried away, it is important to become aware of when this has happened, to discuss the reasons why, to allay anxieties or guilty feelings, and to channel the energy in a positive direction.

Two final points about role reversal and role play

As a general rule, once you have entered the role of another, you should speak in the first person as that other. Questions should be addressed to you as if you were that other, and you should respond in kind. If you wish to come out of role to make an aside comment, you should stand up or move away from the chair to denote you are leaving the role.

Secondly, please remember the often overlooked point that by taking on other roles and points of view, we are doing so based on our own perceptions of that other person. There is no pretence that this is the actual other person. Therefore the insights we gain are just as much about us as they are about the other, and should not be assumed to be an accurate reflection of the actual other. Nevertheless, the insights we gain in role reversal are often of great benefit in helping us understand the other person's perspective.

Figure 1

Facilitator/
Supervisor

One: Outer Face/ Inner World

Aims

- To allow staff to deepen their insight into the offenders' behaviour in the session, and to gain a better understanding of their own reactions, thoughts and feelings.
- To help staff members identify and give voice to their hidden, instinctive and perhaps 'non-professional' responses to what has taken place in a group or individual session.

The technique

This technique draws inspiration from the memorable scene in Woody Allen's film, 'Annie Hall,' in which Woody Allen's character and Annie are having a conversation, and we can read the subtitles that reveal their thoughts as they are speaking. The scene is startling and funny because of the great contrast between the spoken dialogue and the subtitled thoughts. It captures an experience common to us all, which is that in certain circumstances we feel the need to preserve an outer 'mask' to conceal our inner thoughts and feelings - our 'inner world.'

In this technique, two or more chairs are set out, representing all those present in the session. In addition, another chair is placed behind each of the first chairs. We thus have two or more pairs of chairs, each pair having one chair in front of the other. When setting out the chairs, try to take into account the actual positions of the people concerned, for instance whether a particular person usually sits in the same place, or sits slightly away, or even in a corner. (see fig. 1)

In each pair of chairs, the chair in front represents the manner in which that person presented in the session, their behaviour, body language, tone of voice, opinions expressed, etc. This chair is in effect the 'outer face' of the person concerned.

The second chair, the one behind, represents the person's 'inner world.' For the offender, his inner world might, for example, include unspoken thoughts about his offending or his presence in the group, thoughts and feelings about group leaders and other group members, shameful thoughts, fantasies and feelings, and even his positive aspirations. Both his conscious and unconscious processes can be addressed.

For the staff member, their inner world might include feelings of concern, sadness or revulsion, a sense of being frozen and unable to respond, or a desire to 'switch off' and stop listening. All of these are important thoughts and feelings that need to be aired, acknowledged and worked through.

Using this technique, the practitioner sits successively in each of the chairs representing the outer face and inner world for any or all of those present in the session, including themselves (in the case of one-to-one counselling, this will be just the practitioner and the offender). When sitting in a given chair, the worker takes on the role of that person, and gains insight into their point of view. They may also, through the process of taking on both the external presentation and also the inner process, discover what might be the reasons for a particular offender's behaviour in group. For example, in taking on the role of the outer presentation of a particular offender who is openly resistant and antagonistic, the worker may discover while subsequently in role as the offender's inner world that this offender has a very low self-image and a core belief about being worthless, and that he has developed a strategy for protecting this core belief by aggressively intimidating others. With the benefit of this insight, gained from within the role of the offender, the worker may then be able to identify a strategy or intervention that may be more effective for this offender.

By including themselves in this process, practitioners also have the opportunity to revisit their own behaviour and inner processes during the session and to address what was left unsaid beneath their 'professional mask.' Workers can role reverse back and forth between their 'professional mask' and their inner world as often as they require.

Comments

This technique offers an enormous depth of material for consideration, and is suitable for addressing both individual and group work sessions. It is particularly useful in encouraging staff to reveal any persecutory thoughts or feelings they may have in the session. This can be a huge relief to workers who may feel burdened by these responses, or indeed who may deny that they have these thoughts and feelings at all.

Figure 2

Two: A moment from the session: past, present and future

Aim

To examine a particular moment from a session in order to discover some of the underlying dynamics that were positively or negatively affecting the session at that point.

The technique

The staff concerned are asked to create a sculpt, or tableau, of a particular moment in the group session. This may be a moment they found difficult in some way, or it may even be a moment they thought worked particularly well (see fig. 2). The sculpt is created by having staff members take on the roles of those present at the moment in question, and to assume a relatively static pose that reflects the position, posture and attitude of those involved in the interaction. They may also wish to play out, or re-enact, a short sequence from the session.

Once the sculpt is created, staff can shift around the roles they are in, and examine the points of view of various others. They can also use the doubling, or 'thought bubble' technique, whereby they approach another person in the sculpt and, while standing or sitting beside them, attempt to speak the inner thoughts and feelings of this person. As with the first technique, it is important to try to get at the inner world of the various people in the sculpt, to try to discover the concealed processes driving the group interaction.

In the light of the insights gained from this exercise, it is often useful to imagine the next session, and rehearse new possibilities for addressing the group needs and dynamics. Staff can use a round-robin style of rehearsal, with various staff offering differing styles of intervention. Be careful not to let this become a 'my way's better than your way' session. As the rehearsals progress, other staff members can continue to offer inner voice thoughts and feelings, so we hear a running commentary of internal processes as well. Those role playing the group members and group leaders need not accept every comment made by those providing 'thought bubbles', only those that ring true from their perception of the role. In this way, the role play can be a live experiment, and staff will have the opportunity to "discover more about their clients through becoming them" (Hawkins and Shohet, 1989, p. 97) and receive feedback about how different approaches may work.

Comments

This technique is particularly useful in identifying the processes that triggered a particular event or sequence in a session. It is also useful in uncovering hidden alliances in the group and unspoken attractions and antipathy. In those staff teams that feel able to include themselves in the sculpt, there is also a great potential for opening up a deep level discussion about co-working issues.

These first two techniques have a good deal of overlap. The second one differs primarily in that it focuses on specific interactions in the group, and can incorporate moments in which the group was up and active, involved in some activity perhaps, or even on a break in the canteen. The first technique focuses more on a global view of the apparent and concealed dynamics present in the group.

Figure 3

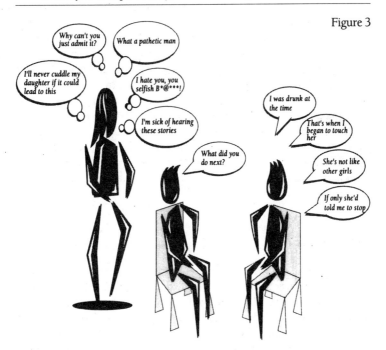

Three: The hypothetical sex offender interview

Aim

To assist practitioners to anticipate and air anxieties about any reactions they may have to working with sex offenders.

The technique

This technique uses the strategy of working at one step removed from an actual situation, at a safe fictional distance. This is meant to make the work safer and more fluid. As most people find it far easier to talk about socially awkward issues if the discussion remains on the level of fiction or the hypothetical, this approach can greatly improve the speed at which hidden anxieties can be surfaced and discussed.

In this technique, two chairs are set up, one representing 'any sex offender' and another representing 'any worker.' Two staff are asked to take these roles, and those remaining are asked to imagine that the offender is describing his offence, or is participating in some other behaviour or group activity which is having an impact on the fictional worker. (see fig. 3)

The other staff members are then asked to come up and provide 'thought bubbles' for the fictional staff member. They do this by standing behind or beside the 'staff member's' chair and speaking their thoughts and feelings. It is also possible to make thought bubble statements for the 'offender' character, but the main emphasis in this technique is on exploring the reactions of the fictional staff member.

Comments

In one-to-one supervision, this technique can be done using just one person role reversing back and forth between the two chairs.

Working at one step removed, on the fictional level, allows staff groups to air and address taboo or difficult subject areas at a safe distance. Many staff members would find it very difficult indeed, perhaps even damaging, to discuss these issues on a personal level, but would nevertheless find it beneficial to discuss them in reference to a hypothetical staff member. Sometimes working at this level can encourage staff groups to become more open on a personal level, but this need not be the intention when using this technique.

Figure 4

Four: One person, many roles

Aim

To encourage a deeper understanding of the offenders we are working with, and also to help identify the abuser, victim and other roles within ourselves.

The technique

Three chairs are arranged in a triangle, facing in. One chair represents the abusive part of a particular offender - the abuser role. The next chair represents the part of that offender that has been hurt or victimised in some way - the victim role. The third chair represents the other roles that the offender has, such as father, husband, worker, brother, son, friend, provider, etc. (see fig. 4).

In the technique, the practitioner successively takes on the role of each part of this offender, and speaks about what this part is like, what drives it and where it comes from. They are meant to consider all of the different roles that the offender has, in addition to being an offender. They can also consider how the various parts are related to each other.

As an option, if the staff members feel able to discuss matters on a personal level, they can consider what they share in common with the offender's experience. They might discuss, for example, a time when they have been abusive in any context, and also a time when they have been oppressed or victimised. As an extension of such a discussion, staff may even wish to take the three chairs for themselves and their own roles.

Comments

This technique uses role theory (Moreno, 1993) as the basis for exploration of the roles we hold within ourselves. One of the advantages of looking at offenders in terms of the many roles they possess is the possibility of harnessing their positive, creative and healthy roles (if they exist) to help them make progress. For example, an incest abuser who is also a reliable employee may be encouraged to show the same diligence in his process of change as he does in the workplace. He can use the efficacy of the one role to influence the efficacy of his more fragile, developing roles. The same may apply to practitioners.

Figure 5

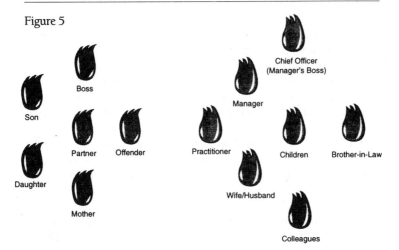

Five: Social networks

Aim

To deepen the practitioner's understanding of how the offender's network of contacts with others, and indeed their own social network, impact on their interactions with offenders.

The technique

Hawkins and Shohet (1989) have called this technique the 'Brandenburg Concerto.' In the technique, first identify a particular client, and then set out chairs or objects to represent the roles of various other key figures in the offender's network of contacts, or social system. These may include the offender's partner, children, parents (alive or deceased), neighbours, boss, friend, publican, victim(s), pets, etc. After the various roles are assigned for the offender's social system, the practitioner then does the same for their own social system. This may include, for example, their manager, their colleagues, the public at large, their family and friends, etc. (see fig. 5)

A short scene is then played, with all those 'present' listening in on the conversation between the staff member and the 'offender.'

In one-to-one supervision, this conversation can take place using role reversal back and forth between the offender and the worker. Each person represented by a chair or object is then asked to respond from their point of view. This may be done through further role reversals, or if there are enough people present the roles can be played by others present. So we may hear, for example, an offender's mother saying that he 'should not let those people (the workers) mess with your head.' Similarly, we may hear the staff member's brother-in-law offering advice such as 'You should stop working with those perverts; it's making you paranoid.' More ominously, we may hear the staff member's manager pressuring them to take on an increased work load because of staff shortages or budget cut backs.

In this way, practitioners are encouraged to consider the interactions they have with offenders in the broader context of social networks on both sides of the equation. They can gain insight into the forces outside of the session which are serving to support or undermine the offender's progress and their own proficiency.

Comments

A useful variation of this technique is to include the worker's ideal, wisest imaginable supervisor (either fictional or real) represented by a chair. In sitting in this chair and taking on the role of the wise supervisor, the worker can often arrive at surprising insights about their interactions in the sessions (Morrell, 1998).

Figure 6

Six: Objects and empty chairs

Aim

To allow the practitioner to address unspoken material, and to rehearse future sessions.

The technique

This technique is best used in one-to-one supervision formats or when the practitioner is alone, and can address work done in either individual or group settings.

In this technique, the practitioner uses one or more empty chairs to represent the offender(s) in the session, and possibly also their co-workers, if any. The practitioner can make statements to these chairs, saying perhaps what can not be spoken, or what they wish they had said at the time. Through a series of role reversals in which they sit in the various chairs and speak from the points of view of those 'present', the practitioner is encouraged to gain a deeper understanding of these others. They can then move on to rehearse various options and strategies of approach for future sessions. (see fig. 6)

In a similar technique, the practitioner can use objects in the room or even a set of marbles, buttons or stones to represent the offender(s) in the session and their co-workers, if any. Rather than having to move from seat to seat, the practitioner can move from object to object, or even simply hold up or touch the various objects as if they were in a sand tray, and speak from their point of view. This simple method of taking others' roles can be highly effective and direct as a way for the practitioner to gain insight into their clients' and co-workers' points of view. And just as with the use of empty chairs, the practitioner can rehearse the upcoming sessions using objects just as easily as empty chairs.

A final note

For those individuals and teams wishing to develop supervision policy and practice, a good place to start would be by reading Hawkins and Shohut (1989) and Swain (1995).

Acknowledgements

The author gratefully acknowledges the assistance of Alyson Coupe, Sally Brookes, Mark Robinson and Vivienne Cole in the production and editing of this chapter. Thanks also to Susie Taylor for her consultation and guidance, and for suggesting the subtitle analogy from 'Annie Hall.'

References

Abel, G.G. et. al. (1985) *Sex Offenders: Results of assessment and recommendations for treatment*. Toronto: G and M Graphic.

Abel, G.G., Becker, J.V., Cunningham-Rathner, J., Rouleau, J., Kaplan, M. and Reich, J. (1986) *The Treatment of Child Molesters: A manual*. New York: SBC-Tm.

Abel, G.G., and Rouleau, J. (1990) The Nature and extent of sexual assault. in W.L. Marshall, D.R. Laws and H.E. Barbaree (eds) *Handbook of Sexual assault: Issues. Theories and treatment of offenders*. New York: Plenum.

Abel, G.G., Blanchard, E.B. and Barlow, D.H. (1981) Measurement of arousal in several paraphilias: The effects of stimulus modality, instructional set and stimulus content on the objective. *Behavioral Research and Therapy*, 19, pp.25-33

ACOP (1992) *The Management of Work With Sex Offenders*. Association of Chief Officers of Probation

ACOP (1994) *Guidance on the Management of risk and Public Protection, Position Statement*. Association of Chief Officers of Probation

ACOP (1996) *Community Based Interventions with Sex Offenders Organized by the Probation Service: A survey of current practice*. Association of Chief Officers of Probation

Ageton, S. (1983) *Sexual Assault amongst Adolescents*. Lexington, MA: Lexington Books

Bagley, C. and King, K. (1991) *Child Sexual Abuse. The search for healing*. London: Routledge

Baker, A. and Duncan, S. (1985) Child Sexual Abuse. Child *Abuse and Neglect*, 9, pp.457-467

Barbaree, H. and Marshall, W. (1988) Deviant sexual arousal, offence history and demographic variables as predictors of re-offence among child molesters. *Behavioural Sciences and the Law*, 6, pp.267-280

Barker, M. and Beech, A. (1992) Sex Offender Treatment Programmes: A Critical Look at the Cognitive-Behavioralist Approach. Paper to British Psychological Society Conference, Harrogate

Barker, M. and Morgan, R. (1993) *Sex Offenders: A framework for the evaluation of community-based treatment.* London: Home Office.

Barker, M. (1996) What works with sex offenders. in G. McIvor (ed) *Working with Offenders.* London: Jessica Kingsley

Bateson, G. (1972) *Steps to an Ecology of Mind.* New York: Balantine Books.

Bateson, G. (1980) *Mind and Nature: A necessary unity.* New York: Bantam Books

Bays, L. and Freeman-Longo, R. (1989) *Who am I and Why am I in Treatment. Understanding my cycle of problem behaviors: A guided workbook for clients in treatment.* Vermont: Safer Society Press.

Beckett, R., Beech, A., Fisher, D. and Fordham, A.S. (1994) *Community-Based Treatment For Sex Offenders: An evaluation of seven treatment programmes.* London: HMSO

Bentovim, A., Elton, E., Hildebrand, J., Tranter, M. and Vizard, E. (1988) *Child Sexual Abuse within the Family.* London: Butterworth

Bentovim, A., Elton, E., Hildebrand, J., Tranter, M. and Vizard, E. (1988) *Child Sexual Abuse within the Family: Assessment and treatment. The work of the Great Ormond Street Sexual Abuse Team.* Bristol: J.Wright

Blatner, A. (1973) *Acting In: Practical applications of psychodramatic methods.* New York: Springer Publishing

Brearley, C.P. (1982) *Risk and Social Work.* London: Routledge & Kegan Paul.

Briggs, D., Doyle, P., Gooch, T. and Kennington, R. (1998) *Assessing Men who Sexually Abuse: A Practice Guide.* London: Jessica Kingsley

Carey, C.H. and McGrath, R.J. (1989) Coping with Urges and Craving. in D.R. Laws (ed) *Relapse Prevention with Sex Offenders.* New York: Guilford Press

Chaney, E.F., O'Leary, M.R. and Marlett, G.A. (1978) Skill training with alcoholics. *Journal of Consulting and Clinical Psychology,* 46

Cook, M. and Howells, K. (1981) *Adult Sexual Interest in Children.* New York: Academic Press.

Crittenden, P. (1988) Family and dyadic patterns of functioning in mal-treating families. in K. Browne, C. Davies and P. Stratton (eds) *Early Prediction and Prevention of Child Abuse.* Chichester: Wiley & Sons

Dale, P., Davies, M., Morrison, T. and Waters, J. (1986a) *Dangerous Families: Assessment and treatment of child abuse.* London: Tavistock.

Dale, P., Waters, J., Davies, M., Roberts, W. and Morrison, T. (1986b) The towers of silence: Creative and destructive issues for therapeutic teams dealing with sex offenders. *Journal of Family Therapy*, 8, pp.1-25

DeShazer, S. (1984) *Keys to Solution in Brief Therapy*. New York and London: Norton.

DeShazer, S. (1989) Wrong map. Wrong territory. *Journal of Marital and Family Therapy*, 15, pp.117-121

De Young, M. (1982) *The Sexual Victimization of Children*. Jefferson, NC: McFarland.

Dietz, C.A. and Craft, J.L. (1980) Family dynamics of incest: A new perpective. *Social Casework*

Douglas (1992) quoted in Morrison, T. (1997) Managing risk: Mission impossible. Paper to NOTA Conference, Southampton

Driver, E., and Droison, A. (1989) *Child Sexual Abuse. Feminist perspectives*. London: Macmillan

Eldridge, H (1997) *Maintaining Change. A personal relapse prevention manual*. London: Sage.

Faller, K.C. (1989) *Child Sexual Abuse. An inter disciplinary manual for diagnosis, case management and treatment.*. London: Macmillan

Faller, K.C. (1990a) *Understanding Sexual Maltreatment*. Beverly Hills, CA: Sage.

Faller, K.C. (1990a) *Child Sexual Abuse. New Theory and Research*. London: Macmillan Education Ltd.

Farmer, E. and Pollock, S. (1998) *Sexually Abused and Abusing Children in Substitute Care*. Chichester: John Wiley.

Finkelhor, D. (1984) *Child Sexual Abuse: New theories and research*. New York: Free Press, Macmillan

Finkelhor, D. (1986) *A Sourcebook on Child Sexual. Abuse* Beverly Hills, CA: Sage.

Fisher, D. and Howard (1993) The Assumptive Stance. Workshop at NOTA Conference, Warwick

Fordham, A.S. (1992) Evaluating Sex Offender Treatment Programmes. Paper to British Psychological Society Conference, Harrogate.

Freud, A. (1981) A psychoanalyst's view of sexual abuse by parents. in P. Mrazek and M. Kemp. *Sexually Abused Children and Their Families*. Oxford: Pergamon

Friday, N. (1976) *My Secret Garden: Women's sexual fantasies*. London: Quartet.

Frosch, S. (1987) Issues for men working with sexually abused children. *British Journal of Psychotherapy*, 3, 4

Furby, L., Weinrott, M.R. and Blackshaw, L. (1989) Sex offender recidivism: A review. *Psychological Bulletin,* 105, pp.3-30

Furniss, T. (1991) *The Multi-professional Handbook of Child Sexual Abuse.* London: Routledge.

Gebhard, P., Gagnan, J. and Pomery, W. (1965) *Sex Offender: An analysis of types.* New York: Harper Row

Gibbens. T.C.N., Soothill, K.L. and Way, C.K. (1978) Sibling and Parent Incest Offenders, *British Journal of Criminology,*18

Gibbens. T.C.N., Soothill, K.L. and Way, C.K. (1981) Sex offences against young girls: A long-term record study, *Psychological Medicine,* 11, pp.351-357

Giller, H. et al (1992) *The Effectiveness of Child Protection Procedures in Four ACPC Areas.* Cheshire: Social Information Systems

Gocke, B. (1991) *Tackling Denial in Sex Offenders: A therapeutic dilemma exacerbated by the criminal justice system.* Norwich: University of East Anglia Social Work monographs.

Gocke, B. (1995) Working with People who have committed sexual offences: What values underpin the behaviour and what value base are we using in attempting to address it? in B. Williams (ed) *Probation Values.* Birmingham: Venture

Gocke, B. and Donaghy, E. (1995) Risk Assessment Format - Sexual Abuse in Family Situations: Interventions training packages.

Gocke, B. and Markham, L. (1997) *Risk Assessment Format for Sexually Abusive Behaviour.* Doncaster: South Yorkshire Probation

Goddard, C. and Hiller, P. (1993) Child sexual abuse: Assault in a violent context. *Australian Journal of Social Issues,* 28, 1, pp.20-33

Grant, D. (1998) *Supervising Sex Offenders in the Community.* Unpublished PhD Thesis. Hull: University of Hull.

Groth, N. (1979) *Men Who Rape: The psychology of the offender.* New York: Plenum Press

Hanks, H. and Hobbs, C. (1993) Failure to thrive: A model for treatment. in C. Hobbs and J. Wynne (eds) *Balliere's Clinical Paediatrics.* London: Balliere Tindall

Hawkins, P. and Shohet, R. (1989) *Supervision in the Helping Professions.* Buckingham: Open University Press

Herman, J. (1981) Father-daughter incest signs. *Journal of Women in Culture and society,* 2, 4, pp.735-75

Hooper, C.A. (1992) *Mothers Surviving Child Sexual Abuse.* London: Routledge

Houston, G. (1990) *Supervision and Counselling.* London: The Rochester Foundation

Hudgins, K. (1998) *The Centre for Experiential Learning Newsletter,* Winter. Charlottesville, Va.: The Centre for Experiential Learning

Hudson, S.M. (1992) Sexual deviance. in P.H. Wilson (ed) *Principals and Practice of Relapse Prevention.* New York: Guildford Press.

Hudson, S.M. (1994) in Seidman, B.T., Marshall, W.L., Hudson, S.M. and Robertson, P.J. An examination of intimacy and loneliness in sex offenders. *Journal Of Interpersonal Violence,* 9, 4, pp.518-534

Jefferies, J. (1991) What we are doing here is defusing bombs. in P. Holmes & M. Karp (eds) *Psychodrama: Inspiration and technique.* London: Tavistock/ Routledge

Jefferies, J. (1996) A psychodrama perspective. in C. Cordess & M. Cox (eds.) *Forensic Psychotherapy.* London: Jessica Kingsley

Jeffreys, S. (1985) *The Spinster and her Enemies.* London: Pandora.

Jenkins, A. (1990) *Invitations to Responsibility: The therapeutic engagement of men who are violent and abusive.* Adelaide: Dulwich Centre Publications

Kemshall, H. (1996) *A Review of Research on the Assessment and Management of Risk and Dangerousness: Implication for policy and practice in the probation Service.* London: HMSO

King, M. and Trowell, J. (1992) *Children's Welfare and the Law. The limits of legal intervention.* London: Sage

Knopp, F.H. (1984) *Retraining Adult Sex Offenders: Methods and models.* Vermont: Safer Society Press

Langan, M. and Day, L. (1992) *Women, Oppression and Social Work. Issues in anti-discriminatory practice.* London: Routledge

Langevin, L. (1990) Sexual anomalies and the brain. in W. Marshall et al *Handbook of Sexual Assault.* New York: Plenum.

Lazarus (1976) in C. Hollin and R. Howells *Clinical Approaches to Sex Offenders and Their Victims.* New York: John Wiley

Macleod, M. And Saraga, E. (1988) *Challenging the orthodoxy: Towards a feminist theory and practice, Feminist Review,* 2

Marques, J.K., Day, D.M., Nelson, C., Miner, M.H. and West, M.A. (1991) *The Sex Offender Treatment and Evaluation Project: Fourth Report to the State Legislature in Response to PC 1365.* California: Department of Mental Health

Marques, J.K. and Nelson, C. (1989) Elements of High Risk Situations for Sex Offenders. in D.R. Laws (ed.) *Relapse Prevention with Sex Offenders.* New York: Guilford Press.

Marshall, W.L. (1996) Key Note Address to NOTA Conference.

Marshall, W.L. and Barbaree, H.E. (1990) Outcome of comprehensive cognitive-behaviour treatment programmes. in Marshall, W.L., Laws, D.R. and Barbaree, H.E. (eds) *Handbook of Sexual assault: Issues. Theories and treatment of Offenders.* New York: Plenum

Marshall, W.L., Barbaree, H.E. and Christophe, D. (1986) Sexual offenders against female children: Sexual preferences for age of victims and type of behaviour. *Canadian Journal of Behavioral Sciences,* 18, pp.424-439

McCluskey, U. and Bingley Miller, L. (1995) theme-focused family therapy: The inner emotional world of the family. *Journal of Family Therapy*

Miller, W.R. and Rollnick, S. (1991) *Motivational Interviewing. Preparing people to change addictive behaviour.* New York: Guildford Press.

Mischel, W. (1973) Toward a Cognitive Social Learning Reconceptualization of Personality. *Psychological Review,* 80, pp.252-283

Moore, B. (1997) *Risk Assessment: A practitioner's guide to predicting harmful behaviour.* London: Whiting & Birch

Moreno, J.L. (1993) *Who Shall Survive? Foundations of sociometry, group psychotherapy and sociodrama.* McLean, VA: American Society of Group Psychotherapy and Psychodrama

Morrell, C. (1998). From workshop presented at 1998 British Psychodrama Association Conference

Morrison, T. (1995) *Staff Supervision in Social Care.* London: Pitman Publishing

Morrison, T., Erooga, M. and Becket, R.C. (!994) *Sexual offending Against Children. Assessment and treatment of male abusers.* London and New York: Routledge.

Morrison, T., and Print, B. (1995) *Adolescent Sex Abusers: An overview.* Hull: NOTA.

Nelson, S. (1987) *Incest: Facts and myth.* London: Stramullion Co-op

Nichols, H.R., and Molinder, I. (1984) *Multiphasic Sex Inventory Manual.* (Available from Nichols and Molinder, 437 Bowes Drive, Tacoma WA 98466, USA)

Parton, N. (1991) *Governing the Family: Child care, child protection and the state.* Basingstoke: Macmillan

Pithers, W.D. (1990) Relapse prevention with sexual aggressors: A method of maintaining therapeutic gain and enhancing external supervision. in W.L. Marshall, D.R. Laws and H.E. Barbaree (eds) *Handbook of Sexual Assault: Issues, theories and treatment of the offender.* New York: Plenum

Pithers, W.D., Buell, M.M., Kashima, K., Cumming, G. and Beal, L. (1987) Precursors to Relapse of Sexual Offenders. Paper to the first meeting of the Association for the Advancement of Behaviour Therapy for Sexual Abusers, Newport: Oregon

Pithers, W.D. and Cumming, G.F. (1989) Can relapses be prevented? Initial outcome data from the Vermont Treatment Programme for sexual aggressors. in D.R. Laws (ed.) *Relapse Prevention with Sex Offenders*. New York: Guilford Press

Pithers, W.D., Cumming, G.F., Beal, L.S., Young, W. and Turner, R. (1989) Relapse prevention: A method for enhancing behavioural self-management and external supervision of the sexual aggressor. in B. Schwartz (ed) *Sex Offenders: Issues in treatment*. Washington DC: National Institute of Corrections

Pithers, W.D., Marques, J.K., Gibat, C.C. and Marlatt, G.A. (1983) Relapse prevention with sexual aggressives: A self-control model of treatment and maintenance of change. in J.G. Greer and J.R. Stuart (eds) *The Sexual Aggressor: Current perspectives on treatment*. New York: Van Nostrand Reinhold

Plummer, K. (1981) Paedophilia: Constructing a sociological baseline. in M. Cook and K. Howells (eds) *Adult Sexual Interest in Children*. London: Academic Press.

Priestley, P., and McGuire, J. (1985) *Offending Behaviour*. Batsford Academic

Prochaska, J. and Di Clemente, C. (1982) Transtheoretical therapy: Towards a more integrated model of change. *Psychotherapy: Theory, Research and Practice*, 19, 3

Quinsey, V.L., Harris, G.T. and Rice, M.E. (1995) Actuarial prediction of sexual recidivism. *Journal of Interpersonal Violence,* 10, pp.85-105

Richards, L.A. and Sharkey, P. (1996) Gender Issues in Co-Working. Paper to Nota Conference.

Rush, F. (1980) *The Best Kept Secret: Sexual abuse of children*. New York: McGraw-Hill.

Ryan, G., Davis, J., Miyoshi, T., Lane, S. and Wilson, K. (1987) Getting at the facts: The First Report from the Uniform Data Collection System, *Interchange*, June 5th

Ryan, G. and Miyoshi, T. (1990) Summary of a pilot follow-up study of adolescent sexual perpetrators after treatment, *Interchange*, January 6-8th

Ryan, G. and Lane, S. (1991) *Juvenile Sex Offending. Causes, consequences and correction*. Lexington, MA: Lexington Books

Salter, A. (1988) *Treating Child Sex Offenders and Victims. A practical guide.* Newbury Park, CA: Sage

Shaw, R. (1978) The persistent sexual offender - control and rehabilitation: A follow-up. *Probation Journal*, pp.61-63

Sheath, M. (1990) Confrontative work with sex offenders: Legitimized nonce bashing? *Probation Journal*, 37, 4

Shergill, M., and Khan, A. ((1997) Working with diversity in the management of sex offenders: Black perspectives. *NOTANews*, 21, pp.36-38

Skuse, D. et al (1997) cited in A.Bentovim and B. Williams (1998) Children and adolescents: Victims who become perpetrators. *Advances in Psychiatric Treatmen*, 4, pp.101-107

Stephenson, M. (1991) A summary of an evaluation of the Community Sex Offender Programme in the Pacific region. *Forum on Corrections Research*, 3, 4, pp.25-30

Stratton, P. and Hanks, H. (1991) Incorporating curricularity in defining and classifying child maltreatment. *Human Systems*, 2, pp.181-200

Swain, G. (1995) *Clinical Supervision: The principles and process.* London: Health Visitors' Association

Thornton, D. (1997) Developing Systemic Risk Assessment for Sex Offenders. Address to NOTA Annual Conference, Southhampton, September.

Waterhouse, L. (1993) *Child Abuse and Child Abusers. Protection and prevention.* Research Highlights in Social Work. 24. London: Jessica Kingsley.

Wattem, C. et al (1989) *Child Sexual Abuse. Listening, hearing and validating the experiences of children.* London: Longman.

White, M. (1984) Marital therapy: Practical approaches to longstanding problems. *Australian Journal of Family Therapy*, 5, 1, pp.27-43

White, M. (1986a) Negative explanation, restraint and double description: A template for family therapy. *Family Process*, 22, pp.255-273

White, M. (1986b) Anorexia nervosa: A cybernetic perspective. in J. Elka-Hardway (ed) *Eating Disorders*. Maryland: Aspen

Westwood, S. (1988) Sex offenders need help too. *Social Work Today*, 58, 4, pp.18-19

Wolf, S.C. (1984) A Multi-Factor Model of Deviant Sexuality. Paper to the Third International Conference on Victimology, Lisbon